KEEPING PROMISES

THE CHALLENGE OF A SOBER PARENT

About the book:
Keeping Promises: The Challenge of a Sober Parent is a book for all recovering parents. Both parents and children in a chemically dependent family must work to heal old wounds and create a new environment in the home. This book addresses such parenting issues as false expectations, starting anew, disciplining, communicating feelings, and educating children about alcohol and other drugs.

About the author:
Kay Marie Porterfield is a professional writer and recovering parent who has written extensively about chemically dependent families.

KEEPING PROMISES

THE CHALLENGE OF A SOBER PARENT

KAY MARIE PORTERFIELD

First published December, 1984

ISBN: 0–89486–245–6

Printed in the United States of America

Editor's note:
Hazelden Educational Materials offers a variety of information on chemical dependency and related areas. Our publi-
cations do not necessarily represent Hazelden or its programs, nor do they officially speak for any Twelve Step
organization.

To Mom and Dad
and to Dylan and Walter, who traveled the road with me.

CONTENTS

Introduction 1
Starting Points 7
Taking Inventory 23
How Our Children Learned To Cope 49
The Sobering Reality 73
Creating A New Family Environment 91
Dealing With Feelings 115
Talking With Our Children About Alcohol
    And Other Drugs 135

Introduction

"I've got tons of housework today, Dylan. Why don't you play outside for a while? . . . Wouldn't an overnight at your friend's house be fun? I'll go pack your clothes! . . . You look tired. I know it's an hour before your regular bed time, but I think you should turn in anyway."

During the two and a half year period of his life after I crossed the line between social drinking and alcoholism, I invented many reasons to shoo my preschooler away so I could take refuge in my everpresent bottle of wine "hidden" in the refrigerator behind the cartons of milk and orange juice. I'd made a vow to myself never to drink to the point of inebriation in front of my child.

Before long, I'd broken my promise and couldn't wait until he was out of the house or even out of the room to drink. I needed a *new* set of excuses to cover up my behavior, a litany of denial to hide my drinking from him—from myself. "It's a sour kind of grape juice and I know you wouldn't like it," I warned when he made a move for my glass of chablis. "Mommy has her mind on other things," I explained when I made lunch and the sandwiches turned out to be tinned cat food instead of tuna. I bumped into furniture, walked unsteadily, and dropped everything from full cartons of eggs to the open can of paint I was using to redecorate the living room. "I'm just uncoordinated,"

1

I'd tell him. "In high school I could barely pass gym. Clumsy Mommy!" Both of us would laugh—our laughter was strained.

Even though he was only four, he knew something was terribly wrong. "You used to tell me you were clumsy," he informed me three *sober* years later when he was seven. "I knew you were drinking all along. I wanted you to stop, but I didn't want to hurt your feelings. You know, I loved you even when you were drunk all of the time."

And I loved him all that time too, yet because I was a practicing alcoholic, drinking exerted a stronger pull on my time and energy than my child. I was addicted to alcohol, not my son, and drinking rather than Dylan became my top priority. I delighted in spending time with him—unless it interfered with satisfying my craving for a glass of wine or scotch. I wanted to be the best possible parent I could be for him and I did have my moments—when I wasn't craving a drink, drinking, or reeling with an unbearable hangover. Unfortunately, those moments were rare, fleeting, and unpredictable. Toward the end, they vanished completely.

The week I stopped drinking, I realized in a flash of nearly paralyzing insight that no matter how many bedtime stories I'd stumbled over or batches of cookies I'd baked, I had not been able to provide Dylan with the emotional nurturance, or set the limits he needed during the time when my life centered around drinking. How could I nurture a small child when I despised myself and felt like a miserable failure? How could I establish fair and consistent limits for him when I couldn't stick to the few limits I'd managed to set for myself? The dual task of rebuilding my own life and my relationship with Dylan seemed overwhelming.

One day at a time, I persisted. Slowly at first, I began adapting to life without liquor and I resumed the parenting role I'd abdicated when drinking dictated my actions. No longer able to hide behind the alcohol-induced haze which stood between my child and myself, I saw clearly what had gone wrong, what needed to be done. We *both* persisted, Dylan and I. We argued, cried, talked, and finally were able to laugh and to love fully again.

Our journey has been a difficult one, but well worth the effort. Some days the twists and turns came so fast they made us dizzy. At other times, darkness closed in and we couldn't see the noses in front of our faces. But after a while the road seemed to smooth out, and the good days outnumbered the bad. Every step we took brought us closer to the goal of coming together as a family—one step at a time. It is a journey many recovering parents will take with their children.

This book is intended as a beginning point for recovering alcoholics and other substance abusers who want to take those first uncertain steps with their kids, steps which in time will become confident strides. It grew from my experience as a recovering parent. As I talked with professionals and with other recovering parents, I found I had much to learn. Because recovery is an ongoing process, I still have *more* to learn. Our journey as recovering chemically dependent people and our journey as parents never ends. There's always something new around the next corner.

The pages ahead don't lay out a set itinerary; instead, they are more like a road map. Every one of us starts from a slightly different place. We will take our own unique detours and side trips. Yet even though the routes we take may differ, we are all aiming in the same direction. We share the same destination: becoming better parents.

While many of the suggestions in this book will be helpful to you, others will not be because your own family situation is unique. Some recovering parents find the road easier than others. Quite a few of us will get lost and need to reach out for professional help in order to find our way again. Family therapy makes much more sense than stumbling around in circles. Later on, we'll talk about that in detail.

Since most research to date has centered on recovering alcoholics and their children, I will mention alcoholism frequently. It is important to remember that patterns of alcoholism and other forms of chemical dependency have much in common. Addiction to any mood-altering drug distorts our relationships with our kids to some extent.

There is no way to make vanish the months or years we focused on alcohol or other drugs instead of our children, no way to erase the hours and days we forgot how to be parents to our kids and couldn't have managed the job even if we'd remembered it was ours. Looking back too much, feeling guilt over what we can't undo, makes us forget where we're going. We can't change the past. We *can* change the ways in which we relate to our kids today and change the future course of our lives and theirs.

Before that can happen, though, recovering parents need to do some homework. Through the first three steps of Alcoholics Anonymous we acknowledged our alcoholism or other drug addiction and believed there was hope for us. We could recover, but not by dint of our willpower alone. We took a leap of faith by entrusting ourselves to a Higher Power.

The next four steps involve facing ourselves and our negative behaviors and asking the help of a Higher Power to remove them.

By the time you read this, you've probably faced your flaws and shortcomings, are attending A.A. meetings, have admitted you're an alcoholic in those meetings, and are ready to change, to let go of the old ways of thinking and acting. The very fact that you're reading this indicates you are willing to make amends as set forth in the Eighth Step. Now it's time, with the help of your Higher Power, to make those amends, remembering that the Higher Power can't help if you don't cooperate.

The past may have affected us, but we aren't slaves to it. We can change. We will recover. That simple bit of wisdom is one of the most valuable legacies we can give to our children. Starting here. Starting now. We're ready to move on.

ONE

Starting Points

"I have two children, a boy and a girl who are both in their middle teens. Most of the time when they were growing up, I was too busy drinking to even notice them. Now I see them and I think to myself, these kids are strangers; I hardly know them. Sometimes I think I've blown my chances as a father because there's so little time left with them."

"My daughter's fourth grade teacher keeps calling me in for conferences about her behavior. I know that part of her problem is an indirect result of my tranquilizer addiction. For the past three years I was physically present in her life, but my mind was in outer space. Sometimes she says she hates me and I don't blame her for that. I want to cope, but where do I begin?"

"I feel so guilty when I look back at the ways I've treated my children. There were many nights I'd come home from work, start dinner, and then retreat to my bedroom to drink myself into oblivion. When they bothered me, I'd rage at them. I want to make it up to them, now that I'm sober, but motherhood still seems like a constant battle. They resent my A.A. meetings and there are times I wonder if they're not trying to drive me to drink again."

You Aren't Alone

According to Migs Woodside, executive consultant to the New York Governor's Conference on Children of Alcoholics, there are over seven million kids below the age of 20 who live with at least one alcoholic parent. National Institute on Alcohol Abuse and Alcoholism figures estimate there are as many as 29 million children of alcoholics in the U.S. Tragically, many of their parents won't face the sobering truth about their dependency. Quite a few of these children will reach adulthood never knowing exactly why Dad could be loving one minute and verbally abusive the next, why Mom drank or took tranquilizers and acted as if they were invisible. Too many will blame themselves for a family life that wasn't the best.

Your children can look forward to a brighter future because you, a recovering alcoholic, have recognized your addiction and are doing something about it! Thousands of recovering alcoholics have children who need healing every bit as much as their parents do. Recognizing that our addiction has touched our children's lives in a negative way and deciding to do what we can to help them recover as we are doing is a courageous and necessary step.

Some of us didn't abuse alcohol, but instead, were dependent on other drugs: tranquilizers, pain-killers, or amphetamines. Others were multiple chemical abusers. One of the biggest things we share in common is that we are on the road to recovery and we want to bring our children along with us. When our kids live with us, we confront the job of changing the negative ways of coping and doing things which were set up within our families while we were chemical abusers. Others do not currently live with their children. These parents face the job of repairing relationships over long distances or with adult children who have flown the nest.

All recovering alcoholics and other substance addicts have a mandate to practice the Eighth Step in the Alcoholics

8

Anonymous program: to make direct amends to all people we have harmed wherever possible. We and our children all stand to benefit when we give them high priority as we begin making amends. We can't undo our alcoholism; we can enable our relationships with our children to grow and flourish starting today.

The seeds have already been planted. "I loved you even when you were drinking." My own son's words express the feelings of most children of alcoholics. It is important to remember that there were positive feelings and good times even when we were so absorbed in our drugs of choice that we weren't the best of parents. Even though their trust for us may have been eroded, their feelings bottled up, and open communication impossible, the basic parent/child bond we share with our children still remains, no matter how frail and tenuous it may have become.

The job now is to take a long and hard look at the weeds in the family garden—hurt feelings, anger, pain, alienation, and sadness—which may still be choking our childrens' growth and our growth as parents. Once we identify our problems and face them, we can deal with them one by one and slowly eliminate the weeds so our relationship with our kids will blossom.

The task at hand isn't easy! In fact it's downright overwhelming, especially at a time when we aren't quite secure in our newfound sobriety. It's difficult enough to take on responsibility for ourselves without adding the role of parent to our job description. When we look back at our record as parents in the past, we can easily become depressed. It is tempting to collapse under this burden of guilt and give up. But turning our backs on our children, returning to the bottle or the other drugs to avoid a painful past doesn't solve the problem of how to be a parent. Our kids' needs don't vanish because we choose to ignore them!

There are other days when we lack the courage to stand up to the testing our kids can give us. Their misdeeds seem like a personal affront. We become angry and frustrated and decide that perhaps the children are deliberately attempting to sabotage our sobriety.

We become impatient. We want a miracle and we want it to happen *now!* Why can't we become like one of those perfect television sitcom families who solve their troubles in half an hour with time out for commercials? Is it because we're recovering alcoholics? Is it because we're failures? We forget that no real family is perfect—even families in which alcoholism and substance abuse aren't issues, have hassles. Some of those problems are more severe and intense than the ones we face.

When recovering parents feel overcome with self doubts and overwhelmed with despair, it's time to go back over those first Seven Steps and get a firmer grasp on faith in a Higher Power. No recovering parent travels the road alone. There's always help. It's up to us to ask for it.

Just What Lies Ahead Of Us?

We will listen to and learn to accept our children's embarrassment and anger at our "under-the-influence" behavior for the first time. Because we can no longer comfort ourselves with the security blanket of denial, some of the revelations we hear will be painful:

> *"You never kept any of your promises. You said you'd come to the school play, but you got drunk and never showed up."*

> *"I was so mad at you I could have killed you, the night you picked my friends and me up and you'd been drinking. They told their parents, and after that they could never ride in our car or even come to our house again."*

> *"At night I'd lay in my bed and hear you and dad arguing. I'd be crying and wishing I'd never been born."*

Quite a few of us will struggle to stabilize the balance of power in our homes. While we were actively chemically dependent, we often expected our offspring to parent us and take on adult roles in our homes. Frequently our kids did the chores we were unable to do, gave us emotional support, and helped us hide our addiction from the outside world. When we say we want to be in charge from now on, we upset the order we've established by default. Some of our children have never experienced a sober parent. The new image we want to project may take some time for them to get used to. Some kids feel demoted and they're afraid we don't need them any more. They can resent being told what to do. Forced in the past to take on more responsibility for their age than was necessarily a good thing, they may need to learn how to be children again.

Frequently as we recover, we need to help our children learn new ways of behaving. It might have seemed very appropriate for a child to whine, throw temper tantrums, or steal in order to get our attention while we were obsessed with drinking. Even negative attention was better than none. Some of us have kids who strove to become perfect in order to win our love and approval away from the bottle. Other children withdrew into a world of their own to protect themselves from being hurt by our chemical dependency. When we stop using alcohol or other drugs, our children don't automatically possess a new set of coping skills which are appropriate to the here and now. They must learn their new, more appropriate, behaviors just as we are learning ours.

We face learning how to be more consistent as we discipline our children. When we were in the midst of alcohol or other drug dependency we experienced mood swings. A child who turned the T.V. set up too loud might be yelled at, spanked, nagged, ignored, or reasoned with, depending on how we felt at the moment. How we reacted, more often than not, depended on our stage of intoxication. When we felt guilty about ignoring our kids or being too harsh, we might even have bent over backwards to laugh off or praise the same behavior we'd hit the roof about the day before. Our children found it nearly impossible to predict how we would react, so it was difficult for them to guess our expectations for their behavior, let alone live up to them. Frequently they stopped trying. It was impossible to win at a game where the rules constantly changed.

Now we need to establish consistently fair rules and predictable consequences for times when those rules are broken. As we grow more secure in the knowledge that we can manage our lives, we can help our kids gain more control over their own behavior. By setting and enforcing fair limits for our kids, we help them become winners, something they couldn't be when family rules changed constantly.

Some recovering parents disciplined with physical force, verbal violence, or a combination of both while under the influence of alcohol or other drugs. Although alcohol and other drugs do not cause family violence or emotional abuse, there is a relationship between the two. As many as a third of physical child abuse reports involve a drinking parent. It is critical to learn other, more effective ways of helping children behave. If such incidents were a repeated occurrence, it would be wise to seek help from a family professional as you try to make changes in the way you deal with anger and child discipline.

Many of us will be startled, as we become accustomed to a chemical-free life, at just how manipulative our kids may have become. Yet we often lied, manipulated, denied, and covered up in order to protect our dependency. We've set an example of how *not* to be direct and sometimes we've reinforced it in our dealings with our children. "I never knew what my mom would do when I asked her for my allowance," admits a thirteen-year-old. "She might cry and tell me she was broke or maybe yell at me for what seemed like forever. It was easier on everybody if I just took it from her purse."

By the same token, as chemically dependent people,

we've too often run from our feelings and hidden in a liquor bottle or a pill bottle, rather than coping directly with life. Even though our children may not be chemically dependent themselves, chances are they have learned by our example that open communication and emotional honesty is something to be avoided at all costs. Rather than taking risks and asking for what they need, they may continue to "get around" the recovering parent, to play parents off one another. It is possible they don't see manipulation as something they choose or choose not to do; they may not know there are other alternatives.

Some kids who have lived in an alcoholic family system for a long time may not even know *what* they want from us so it is impossible for them to ask for it, whether it's a hug or a new pair of running shoes. In order to avoid being hurt, they've learned never to get their hopes up. If they don't allow themselves to consciously need anything, then they won't feel crushed when they don't receive anything. Before they can become more assertive and direct we may need to help them get in touch with their feelings and needs.

Successful recovering family members learn how to talk to each other and to listen (even when it hurts to do so). When we begin sharing feelings with our children and encouraging them to share with us, we gain in understanding and foster trust. When we teach kids to be open and direct in getting their needs met and are straightforward about our own needs, we unhook from the denial part of our disease. Sometimes we must start at the very beginning and reassure our kids that it's O.K. to have needs and wants in the first place. Because denial is such an integral part of alcoholism and other drug dependencies, we'll need to keep assuring our children and ourselves that it is O.K. to express feelings and to ask directly for what we want (even though we may not always get it).

Finally, all recovering parents, to some extent, must earn back their childrens' trust. In the past it was impossible for us as practicing alcoholics or chemical abusers to be very predictable or trustworthy. No matter how good my intentions were when I'd make a promise to Dylan to take him to the zoo or even watch T.V. with him, whether or not I followed through depended entirely on my state of intoxication. When he needed to talk with me, he couldn't predict if I'd be grouchy, euphoric, morose, or turning green with a hangover. He had no control over what would happen next because I had no control over my desire for alcohol or over my actions after I drank. With good reason, he learned not to trust me.

As recovering chemical abusers, we begin changing that. Some of us desperately long for our kids to trust us, to treat us as if we've always been as dependable as the Rock of Gibraltar. But we *weren't* very reliable, and trust doesn't come to us instantly. It comes slowly. When we backslide and fall into drinking or other drugs again, the trust we've built with our children takes a backward step right along with our behavior. Trust grows stronger as we and our children grow stronger—one day at a time.

Each Of Us Will Face Unique Challenges

Not all alcoholics and other drug-dependent people are alike, nor are their families identical. They share many thorny family issues in common, yet it stands to reason that each parent will have a slightly different set of challenges to tackle as he or she learns to relate to children in new ways.

Family members who participated in Al-Anon or who formed a support network of caring nonalcoholic adults, either relatives, friends, neighbors, therapists, or teachers, already have a head start on recovery. They've learned how to form relationships which don't focus around substance dependency.

Often out of embarassment and a need to protect an alcoholic or drug dependent parent from the world, children withdraw and shun outside contacts. They may not form close friendships so they won't be in the awkward position of inviting friends home to see Mom or Dad passed out on the sofa. "I used to be involved in church activities," says a fifteen-year-old girl. "But after the youth leader smelled beer on my dad's breath, she acted like she pitied me. I didn't want to show my face around there again and it was easier just to stay home and read or watch T.V. in my room."

Isolated children who have had little or no close contact with others outside their immediate family, may have no idea of how to relate in situations where addiction isn't the central theme. They learn to cope with the alcoholic parent using a set of survival skills which aren't useful during recovery. Even when these children have formed a close relationship with their nonalcoholic parent, chances are most of that parent's energy was devoted to surviving an alcoholic marriage. A good deal of parent/child interaction may have been spent explaining the alcoholic parent's actions or protecting the child from those behaviors. In addition, there may have been silent agreements to cover for the alcoholic parent and not to discuss the alcohol or other drug problem even with family members.

Kids who have only experienced one way of doing things may not even be aware that they and their family *can* change, and our new expectations may be frightening to them. The only family they've seen at close range is one which centered around a chemical dependency problem. Children and adults must be made aware of their options before they can act on them.

Alcoholism counselors who work with women often note the great burden of guilt their clients bear. Most of us were raised to have a good deal of our self-esteem hooked to the role of Mom. When we stop our drinking or other drug use and realize we've slighted our kids in the past, we may feel like non-persons, less than human. We need

15

to remember that parenthood isn't our only role and that our children are separate from us. Even if there were such a thing as a perfect mother, she would have no guarantee that her children would automatically grow up to be perfect adults. A number of factors influence how children grow, factors over which none of us have any control.

During my first few months of sobriety, I found my guilt issues with Dylan intensified because I spent so much time with him. Often, being a mother means there are few chances to get some distance and perspective on the relationship. As a single parent, responsibility weighed heavily on my shoulders. I found I needed to make a conscious effort to take care of myself as well as my son. When I would ignore my own needs out of a sense of guilt, a desire to undo the past, I had little left to give Dylan.

The guilt women feel is often made worse by the fact that society tends to judge an alcoholic female more harshly than an alcoholic male. Because we've been placed on a pedestal and granted the job of moral guardians of society, we have farther to fall when we topple. Even when a recovering woman doesn't blame herself for her alcoholism, she never has to look far to find someone who will ask, "How could you do that to your children?" It is critical to develop the ability to shrug off such comments. Often it helps to remember that the people who make them are frequently ignorant or misinformed about alcoholism and other drug addiction and see those problems as sins or reflections on a woman's moral character. A few have a difficult time thinking of women as human beings at all. You know better. Their attitude is their problem, not yours!

Recovering mothers may want to make some changes in their lives, like sharing housework instead of doing it all themselves, or beginning a career in order to realize their full potential. Sometimes spouses and children may resist. Who *really* wants to do the dishes three nights a week or come home to an empty house now that Mom's going back to school to get a degree in chemical engineering? Conflicts can arise when a recovering Mom becomes more assertive as she tries to take control of her life. The issues involved may range from "talking back" instead of drinking and swallowing anger after an argument to major life changes like getting job training or changing careers. We have it easier when our families emotionally support us, but we need to remember that we can establish support systems outside of our families, as well. A.A., women's groups, and therapy can help make us stronger so that change isn't so difficult.

Many recovering fathers face a different set of issues than their female counterparts. While Dad was drinking he may have withdrawn from his children and had little to do with them. Quite a few fathers drank at bars or "with the boys," coming home only after the kids were asleep. The next morning was spent grappling with a hangover and trying desperately to get ready for work.

Now suddenly Dad's expected to seize control again and be the "man" in the family, the leader to whom everyone looks for guidance. Because he's a man, sometimes his spouse and other family members think Dad should be able to solve the family's problems singlehandedly, without any assistance from the family or outside professionals. Often he buys into that impossible dream himself. If a man or his family sets impossibly high expectations during recovery, the inevitable feelings of failure can be threatening to recovery.

Some recovering fathers discover they crave a warm and nurturing relationship with their children. They want to begin communicating affection as well as negative feelings and to stop being the family tough guy. Since most men aren't raised to be emotional caretakers, Dad may have been physically present but emotionally aloof from his off-

17

spring long before the drinking began. If he's been removed from the inner workings of his family, he may not have the first idea about where to begin.

It can be unsettling when a spouse accustomed to playing both mother and father, or an older child who has filled Dad's or Mom's shoes during the drinking days, refuses to allow a recovering parent even equal partner status in the household. "We've gotten along so far without you, so why should we include you now?" is extremely frightening for a recovering parent to hear. Remember that often such entrenched positions rarely come from malicious motivations. The family members who performed your functions during your drinking days may have a good deal of self-identity tied up in taking over for you. When you reassume your position in the family, you've in effect given them a "pink slip." It may take time for them to feel secure enough about themselves to comfortably give up extra responsibilities. Your understanding is important, but be firmly determined, as well, not to be excluded from family decision making.

Not all of us acted the same when we were drinking. Those of us who played the part of "mean drunk" may need to work through our children's fear and anger toward us. Our kids might have come to look almost completely to our sober spouses for emotional support and guidance. Under these circumstances, often tight coalitions form between the non-alcoholic spouse and the kids. When a parent has reacted angrily in the past to children's demands and requests, those children learn to "walk on eggs." Chances are, they've also choked back a good deal of outrage at the way they've been treated. Hurt feelings and bitterness don't disappear overnight.

If we were "jolly drunks," our job as recovering parents may be a different one. Some chemically dependent parents may have fallen into the role of a combination pal and

Santa to their kids, indulging them and teaming up with them against mean old Mom or Dad who didn't drink too much and who disciplined. "I felt so bad about being a lush, I always tried to take their minds off my condition and make them like me," says a recovering father.

"If my wife said no to an allowance increase, I'd go behind her back and double the kids' allowances. I'd make up for drinking binges by going out and buying extravagant presents for them. Now that it's stopped and I'm not a sugar daddy, I think they resent it. Sometimes I wonder if they'll ever accept me for who I am instead of what I can buy for them, but it's a situation I set up myself."

Forming a parenting alliance with our spouses rather than a buddy conspiracy with our kids may be difficult to accomplish, but it is essential if we are to be good parents and have our children's respect as well as their friendship.

According to a study of children of alcoholics conducted by Claire Wilson and Jim Orford at the Addiction Research Unit of the Institute of Psychiatry in London, it was found that some children felt pity for their drinking parents when they acted depressed. Many children were able to feel close to an alcoholic parent, distancing themselves or feeling anger mainly when that parent was drinking or actually drunk. Others rejected and felt hostile toward their alcoholic parents all the time.

Just as individuals don't react to liquor or other drugs in the same way, each recovering parent had a slightly different chemical dependence style, a pattern which affected the family atmosphere. Some were off in another world while physically present with their kids most of the time. They had a different impact on their children's lives than those who went on binges, sporadically spending time away from home. Some children may not have seen us drinking, only drunk or hung over, and might not connect our problems and those of the family with alcohol at all. Nonetheless, they did see our hangovers and feel the impact of the instability of our lives even if they never guessed the cause.

How long a recovering parent drank to excess and the ages of our kids at the onset of our alcoholism will also shape the tasks which lie ahead of us. Some of us have kids who can remember the good old days before alcohol or other drugs became the sole focus of our lives. At least part of their growth was not influenced by addiction and they have good memories on which to build. Other recovering parents who developed chemical abuse problems before or shortly after the birth of their offspring need to keep in mind that their kids have only known them as chemically dependent people. The new chemical-free you is a big change in their lives.

If we were able to keep our jobs and our families intact, chances are our children have less to work through than children who have experienced an extreme amount of instability. Yet, even recovering parents who have gone through unemployment, divorce, or problems with the law can rebuild their relationships with their kids and create a new environment where their kids can be happy and well-adjusted.

Usually the recovering parent's family members have a vested interest in learning about alcoholism or other drug abuse and in working to make home life better even though there may be some initial resistance to change. Unfortunately, when divorce divides a family there is no guarantee that an ex-spouse will become informed about the disease or try to understand the recovery process.

A few ex-spouses who were enablers before the divorce and who stand to lose something (many times that "something" is control) if sobriety continues, may actively try to sabotage a recovering parent's recovery. When a former spouse wonders why you didn't stop drinking or taking drugs when the marriage was still intact, he or she may be filled with bitterness.

Sometimes that anger takes the form of criticizing the recovering parent to the children, or starting battles over the children which can culminate, as in my own case, in a protracted custody battle. Fortunately, more often than not, judges and custody evaluation teams see alcoholism recovery in a positive light. The fact that you have recognized the problem and are working to solve it is nothing to be ashamed of.

Some divorced recovering alcoholics feel guilt about the marital break-up, especially if drinking was a factor in the rift. Frequently, rather than working through sadness and anger, chemically dependent people put that process on hold. When a recovering parent begins a chemical-free life, the feelings rush back in and demand to be dealt with. Even though the grieving process after divorce may have been delayed by chemical dependency, the pain and the healing still must be dealt with. Now, instead of getting drunk or stoned, a non-custodial parent has to work through the loss of his or her children on a full-time basis. Custodial parents may need to deal with feeling overburdened and sometimes frightened or resentful of all the responsibility they must shoulder.

How we learn to relate with our children, and how we choose to handle the new set of issues which confront our children and ourselves during our recovery process will also depend on the ages of our offspring. Toddlers require a different approach than teenagers. Younger children may have a difficult time verbalizing their feelings. Sometimes it's difficult to communicate our concerns to them with words. Older kids are capable of more understanding, but because they are developing minds of their own, they may verbally disagree with the changes we attempt. Teenagers in the process of defining themselves and pulling away from

Mom and Dad, require still a different approach. Even when the kids have left home and are now adults there is a need to resolve our chemical dependency issues with them. Our choices, too, will depend on our children's personalities and our own. It may take some experimentation, but there is an effective approach that both a recovering parent and the kids feel comfortable with.

These common and individual challenges all add up to a good deal of work ahead. But even though rebuilding relationships with children is neither simple nor easy, the days to come will hold joy as well as sorrow, insight as well as bewilderment. Gradually, your successes will out-number your mistakes as a parent. Some recovering parents start their journey further along the road than others, but nearly everyone reading this book has taken the first step. You stopped drinking.

That, alone, has a major impact on your children, ac-cording to a study conducted by Drs. Rudolph H. Moos and Andrew Billings of the Social Ecology Laboratory at Stanford University. In the families they studied, when the alcoholic parent began recovery their offspring soon experi-enced less depression and anxiety and had fewer night-mares. In addition, psychosomatic problems caused by stress, such as headaches and indigestion, lessened too. Al-though the study was not a long term one, children of recov-ering alcoholics initially compared favorably with children whose parents didn't abuse alcohol. Moos and Billings con-cluded that the stress-related effects of parental alcoholism on children may diminish or go away completely once the parent stops abusing alcohol.

If you've stopped drinking and have a commitment to continue in sobriety, you're already well along the way to becoming the kind of parent you want to be, the kind of parent your children deserve.

TWO

Taking Inventory

Children need many things from their parents to grow strong and straight. Because we live in a less-than-perfect world, no one gets exactly everything they need all the time. As parents, we're sometimes grouchy and tired. Often, taking care of our kids' physical needs, whether it be changing a diaper or earning money to pay for peanut butter and jelly, forces emotional considerations temporarily aside. That happens in the best of families. No matter how hard you try, you'll never be a perfect parent. However, you can become a better parent.

Has your alcoholism irreversibly damaged your children? Absolutely, not! Some researchers have found some children of alcoholics do exhibit some problems. The general prognosis, however, is far from doom and gloom. "Many children of alcoholics seem to do fine," according to psychologist Andrew Billings of the Social Ecology Laboratory at Stanford University. "We need to remember that the subjects of many of the studies done were both children and adult children of alcoholics who showed up in a therapist's office. There needs to be a good deal more study done on those who don't seem to have problems, and to get beyond the notion that a single factor such as parental alcoholism produces the same kind of effect on every child."

Neither does a recovering parent need to fear that being

an alcoholic parent automatically wreaks havoc on his or her relationship with the kids. Researchers Clare Wilson and Jim Orford say this in *The Journal of Studies on Alcohol:* "It would appear that the behavior and personality of both the drinking and nondrinking parent, the sex, age, and temperament of the child, and factors of family structure such as size or parental separation, all play a part in determining the nature of parent-child relationships. Parental alcoholism probably is not in itself highly predictive of the quality of parent-child relationships."[1]

When we were drinking or using drugs, we weren't necessarily bad parents, but our addictions pushed our children's mental health requirements further down on our list of priorities than was optimal. If we were chronic rather than sporadic drinkers, this happened more frequently. Even so, it is a rare parent who has related in a completely negative way to his or her children, a rare parent who, drinking or sober, hasn't contributed in some positive ways to the children's lives. In some cases, others filled the gaps we left in our kids' lives when we were centered around alcohol or other drugs.

Again we need to take inventory of ourselves as suggested in A.A.'s Fourth Step. This time we'll focus on our weaknesses *and* our strengths specifically as parents. Before a recovering parent can make amends, that parent must find out exactly which amends need to be made. In order to do that we'll evaluate ourselves in terms of how well we met our children's emotional needs in several areas.

Each parent who makes this assessment will finish with a different agenda to follow in the coming days. When I looked back at my own parenting during my drinking days, I had to admit that I'd failed to set limits for my son. Other

---

[1] Wilson, Clare and Jim Orford, "Children of Alcoholics: Report of a Preliminary Study and Comments on the Literature," *Journal of Studies on Alcohol,* Vol. 39, No. 1, (1978), pp. 121–142.

recovering parents set limits for their children which were too rigid and unrealistic.

I *did* manage to provide a number of intellectual experiences for him during those early years and much of the time I was there when he needed me. Other parents will be able to look back and find different "pluses" in their past relationships with their children.

A.A.'s "Big Book"[2] advises recovering alcoholics to think of the Fourth Step assessment much like a business inventory: "Taking a commercial inventory is a fact-finding process. It is an effort to discover the truth about the stock-in-trade." That means looking for our good qualities as parents right along with honestly pinpointing our not-so-positive ones.

Of course, any recovering parent is bound to come up with a list of weaknesses. (If you can't find any, you're probably not being honest with yourself!) We'll work hard to make improvements in those areas. It is equally important for us to note our strengths and capitalize on them. They are the solid foundation on which we'll build our relationships with our kids. A fearless and honest inventory gives us a guide of where we need to focus our thoughts and energy as we begin making amends toward our kids. It's a way to find out what we'll need to acquire for our family recovery journey in the days ahead.

The Mental Health Association has devised a list of eight essential ingredients for a child's mental health: love, security, acceptance, control, guidance, independence, protection, and faith. As you read through the checklist which follows, based on those eight ingredients, you might think of other factors which are important to you. Feel free to make note of them. The list is only a basic one. Answer the questions honestly as you try to determine how you

---

[2] *Alcoholics Anonymous,* published by A.A. World Services, New York, N.Y. Available through Hazelden Educational Materials.

rate as a parent in meeting your children's needs in these eight areas.

Remember that no matter how truthful you are, you will still be subjective. Often it's a good idea to have your spouse rate you, using this checklist so you can see if you're being too hard on yourself or if you've missed some important areas your spouse thinks need improvement. Don't be dismayed if, when you compare your two inventories, it appears they were done on two completely different people. You'll be able to pick up on exactly where you and your spouse agree and differ in your perceptions. This knowledge about new ways of looking at yourself can be a starting point for pulling together and parenting as a team.

If your children are old enough, you may want to have them go over the checklist, too. You could be surprised to find their perceptions of what has gone on in the family are very different from yours. If you see yourself as having been too remote from your children's lives and they think you've been intrusive, chances are the truth lies somewhere in the middle. You'll need to compromise on ways of being a family which everyone can live comfortably with most of the time. One hundred percent happiness for every family member one hundred percent of the time is an impossible goal.

Keep in mind that, although you want and need input from your children, they are children and you are their parent. Asking kids to have final say in setting rules and roles in a family means abdicating your job as parent. You might explain to them that you value their opinions and agree to discuss changes you want to make as a parent with them. At the same time, make it clear that as parents, the adults in the family will exercise limits.

Finally, one positive way to gather information and to come together as a family is to have each family member list concrete examples of how well you've been able to meet needs in these areas in the past. If you take the time to jot down specific ways you can improve and ask family members for the same, the criticism you give yourself and hear from others can be put to constructive use rather than demoralizing you to the point of parental paralysis. Too often, vague ambiguities like, "You don't love me enough," or "I wasn't responsible," become stumbling blocks instead of stepping stones, so focus your thoughts on *specific* examples and suggestions.

How Well Have I Met My Children's Needs?

LOVE: (R = Rarely; S = Sometimes; F = Frequently)
R   S   F

___ ___ ___ I showed my children, through words and actions, I loved them and wanted them.

___ ___ ___ I made my children aware I cared what happened to them.

SECURITY:

___ ___ ___ Our home has been a safe place my children could feel secure about.

___ ___ ___ I made certain that either I or another adult would be there for my kids, especially in times of crisis.

___ ___ ___ I kept my promises to my children and have been a person they could count on.

___ ___ ___ I helped my children feel they were a part of our family group and that they belonged.

ACCEPTANCE:

___ ___ ___ Even when I was angry with my kids, I let them know I liked them for themselves.

___ ___ ___ My children knew I accepted them all the time and not just when they were behaving according to my expectations for them.

___ ___ ___ When I disciplined my children I made certain they understood I still approved of them even though I didn't approve of their behavior.

— — — I've respected the fact that my children are unique individuals and I haven't tried to make them over in my ideal image.

— — — I paid attention to their unique qualities and noticed their accomplishments. I praised my children frequently.

— — — I listened to my children's feelings and accepted their right to feelings which were painful to me.

CONTROL:

— — — I set limits for my children about what they were permitted to do.

— — — Those limits were clear to my kids.

— — — When my kids exceeded those limits, I enforced fair and reasonable consequences.

— — — I was consistent.

— — — My children were explicitly aware of what those consequences would be before they exceeded the limits I'd set.

— — — I made it clear to my kids that it was O.K. to feel jealous or angry, but *not* to hurt themselves or others.

GUIDANCE:

— — — I gave my kids friendly help in learning to behave toward people and things.

— — — I showed my children by example how to get along with other people.

— — — My kids knew I would be there ready to listen when they needed advice or help.

— — — I took the time to talk with my children, to hear what they had to say.

INDEPENDENCE:

— — — I encouraged my children to try new things and to grow.

— — — I noticed my children's attempts to meet challenges and take reasonable risks on their own and I made certain to praise them for it.

___ ___ ___ I expressed confidence to my children that they had the ability to do things for and by themselves.

PROTECTION:

___ ___ ___ I kept my children safe from harm.

___ ___ ___ When my kids faced new, frightening, or dangerous situations, I was there to help them.

FAITH:

___ ___ ___ I gave my children a set of moral standards to live by, both in my words and deeds.

___ ___ ___ I fostered my children's belief in the value of kindness, justice, courage, generosity, trustworthiness, and honesty.

* * *

There is no handy, dandy numerical score for this test, no final grade. For many of us that's a good thing! The very nature of alcoholism and other drug addiction makes it difficult, if not nearly impossible, to function well enough to provide some of the items on the checklist. Remove the impact of alcohol or other drugs in our lives and it is much easier to fulfill our roles as parents. Depending on the length of your sobriety, there's a good possibility you'd rate yourself much higher today if you changed the statements to read in the present tense and took the quiz again. You might want to repeat the checklist inventory every few weeks for a while as a way to work A.A.'s Tenth Step: [*We*] *continued to take personal inventory and when we were wrong promptly admitted it.*[3]

Painful as it may be, it is important to see where we've been as parents in order to map a route to where we want

---

[3] *Alcoholics Anonymous,* published by A. A. World Services, New York, NY. Available through Hazelden Educational Materials.

to go. Even though you may not be feeling proud of your past parenting at this stage, you need to remember that few alcoholic or chemical abusing parents could give themselves a high rating no matter how hard they worked at being parents. Neither did you consciously or willfully set out to ignore your children's needs. The very dynamics of alcohol and other drug dependency worked against your ability to parent. How did that happen?

Love. Parents can love their children profoundly, but if those children don't *feel* loved, they grow up lacking. Even when an addicted parent is lavish with hugs, kisses, and verbal affirmations of love, kids can sense that they play second fiddle to alcohol or other drugs in that person's life. "How could I compete?" asked one teenager. The answer is simple: there is no way a child or anyone else can compete with an addict's craving for his or her chemical. Our kids may have mattered very much to us indeed, but our addiction mattered even more. In our lucid moments we could afford to care about what happened to our kids, but much of the time it was a luxury. We were consumed with caring about our next drink.

When Meg, who was eight, would arrive home from school, she'd often find the stereo blaring and her mom dancing around the living room to old Beatles' tunes with a glass of rum and cola in her hand. Most of the time Meg's mom would ask her how her day in school had gone and the two of them would talk for a few minutes. Meg's mom hugged her daughter and told her how much she loved her frequently during these talks, but usually after a few minutes, she'd turn her attention back to drinking and send Meg off. After Meg finished her homework it was time to get supper. By then Mom was too inebriated to cook.

Later in the evening the arguments would come. Usually they began over Meg turning the T.V. set too loud or her request that her mother help her with a school project. Totally out of control, Meg's mother would scream, "If it weren't for you I wouldn't be divorced. After you came along, your father felt trapped and he left us. I quit school to have you, you know. If I'd finished I could have a good job instead of working part-time for slave wages. I hate you! Just leave me alone!" Meg soon learned that her mother's love for her went up and down like a roller coaster. She couldn't count on it, so she withdrew. Naturally, she played along with her Mom when the next day she'd be apologetic, but how could she believe her mother cared about her when, after enough rum and colas, the yelling would invariably begin again?

As the disease of alcoholism or other drug addiction progresses, those who have it turn inward; the only thing which matters is feeding the addiction. While self-loathing grows, the ability to love others and to care about them diminishes.

When Meg's mother was drunk, she had no control over what she said to her daughter. Her resentments grew and were distorted by alcohol until she could no longer contain them and her disappointment about the past spilled all over her child. Meg didn't understand why her mother yelled at her and said she hated her; she only knew she felt completely unloved. Sometimes she felt sorry for her mom and other times she hated her—and she felt very guilty for her anger.

If our children received love, love they could believe in from us or from their other parent or family members, they are fortunate. Often, though, children from alcoholic families are isolated, and the nonalcoholic parent is just as caught up in the family disease as the child. Grandparents and aunts and uncles may be hooked into the denial process. Frequently, teachers, neighbors, and other family outsiders are reluctant to befriend such a child because they don't understand alcoholism and they fear involvement. It is a sad truth that some children from alcoholic homes feel loved by no one.

Security. At forty, Daniel knew he would never be made a partner in the accounting firm where he worked. A heavy drinker, he began drinking more to ease the pain of what he saw as a failure, but soon he was drinking just to get through the day. In the meantime, his wife took an evening job to help with house payments and the college tuition the family would soon be paying for their two teenage children. Many evenings Daniel drank to the point of passing out. When his fifteen-year-old, Deborah, was picked up at the local mall for shoplifting, he couldn't go to the police station and get her for fear he'd be arrested for drunk driving. One night when his son, Tom, was riding in the car with him, the boy became so frightened of his dad's eratic driving that he grabbed the wheel from him and demanded he be allowed to drive. When Daniel refused to comply, the boy walked home.

Because he resented his wife's working, Daniel often picked fights with her. Depending on the amount he'd been drinking, sometimes he'd throw things at her. On one occasion he demolished the bathroom, breaking the medicine cabinet mirrors and ripping the shower curtain before smashing everything in the cabinet against the tile walls. One night in a fit of rage, he removed all the fuses from the outside box before vanishing into the night and not returning home for three days.

Certainly Deborah and Tom's house wasn't a place where they felt secure. They learned to fear for their safety. Because Dad wasn't around in time of crisis and, in fact, caused many crisis situations himself, Deborah began avoiding home in the evening and spending time with a group of peers who constantly got into trouble. They accepted her and made her feel she belonged more than her father did.

When he was sober, Daniel would feel sorry for the fear he'd caused his kids and promise to make it up to them by taking them to baseball games and on camping trips. Often, when the time came to make good on his promises, he was too inebriated to comply. Deborah and Tom learned not to take him at his word. Their world was an unpredictable and sometimes scary place. "The way I lived was like one of those tornado or nuclear war drills we used to have in elementary school," says Tom, now a college junior. "Dad would start acting crazy and it would be time to tuck and duck. When you have to protect yourself from a parent, what kind of a family is that?"

Because Daniel's wife had to work if the children were to go to college, and because she feared her husband was extremely close to losing his job, she wasn't home to serve as a buffer between them and their Dad. When she was in the house, frequently it was Tom who would intervene when her husband threatened her.

When an alcoholic parent's disease begins affecting his or her job, frequently even young children sense impending financial problems and become insecure about how the family will survive. As family friendships with outsiders who aren't heavy users of alcohol or other drugs fall off, the kids pick up on the fact that the family is alone, there is no social support safety net, no place to turn for reassurance or for help.

Family violence may start to occur as the drinking or other drug use increases, and police are called to quell domestic disturbances. Parents deep in the throes of addiction may neglect their younger children's physical needs, abandoning them without supervision for hours at a time, or forgetting to feed them.

Sometimes alcoholism or other drug addiction splits families through divorce when the chemical abuser's spouse leaves, taking the kids. The loss of any parent, even an alcoholic or drug abusing one, causes the insecurity to peak even higher.

When chemical dependency progresses unchecked, panic and uncertainty become the rule rather than the exception for many children. They must depend, to some extent, on a parent who is undependable. Fear becomes all-pervasive, rather than an occasional emotion.

Acceptance. Ben, a fifth grader, is overweight, too fat to play soccer or basketball—the very things his dad wants him to do. When Ben brings home his report card, which is a praiseworthy collection of A's and B's, Dad seems to develop temporary blindness and sees only the D in gym. Then he pours himself a tumbler of scotch, takes a deep breath, and begins his standard lecture about how sports are the most important part of a growing boy's life. "When you were born, I expected you'd play soccer and basketball like I did. Those days when I was on a team were the happiest I've spent. You've disappointed me, Son."

Choking back tears which would prove him even less manly than his dad already thinks him, Ben slinks off to his room, but not before he grabs a bag of chocolate-coated marshmallow cookies from the kitchen cupboard. As he stuffs himself, he wishes his father understood him. He's not interested in sports. He likes computers and building model rockets. If soccer and basketball get people where his dad is now, he'll never go near the playing field! He bets his father wishes he'd never been born.

Half an hour later, his dad stands weaving in the doorway of Ben's room. His eyes fix on the empty cookie bag and he snatches it from his son's hands. "Pig! Fat slob! I'm only trying to do what's good for you and look at what you do. You gorge yourself. Ben, you're going to grow up to be a fat faggot!"

The tears which Ben has been holding back begin rolling down his cheeks.

"Stop your blubbering," his father commands. "You have no right to feel sorry for yourself. Keep that up and I'll really give you something to cry about."

As soon as he's left the room muttering to himself about his son's weight and his lack of coordination, Ben's mom comes in and sits down on the bed beside Ben who has given himself completely to sobbing now. "You've started him up again," she accuses. "If you'd just try to please him more, he wouldn't get so angry. Now he'll be ranting and raving all night."

"What do you want me to do," Ben hurls back, "flunk school? Lift weights? Why don't you just trade me in for another kid?"

Unless Ben is exactly the kind of person his dad wants him to be, he knows his father doesn't accept him. No matter how hard he tries to please him, he'll always disappoint him. To his dad, Ben's unique accomplishments and interests are a slap in the face, proof that his son isn't everything he wants him to be. In the meanwhile, Ben's mother gives him even more responsibility to be someone he isn't when she blames him for her husband's drinking and his drunken verbal insults. The child has failed them both and he's learned to turn to food as comfort against his failures, much as his dad nurses a glass of scotch to console himself for his sedentary job, his aging body, and his "dull" life.

Many chemically dependent parents are all too familiar with failure. Often in the past, we drank in order to feel better because we didn't measure up to the standards we'd set for ourselves. We weren't beautiful or handsome enough. We weren't attractive enough to the opposite sex. We weren't named best player of the year or given the career promotions we thought we deserved. We were misunderstood. No one really accepted us. We couldn't accept ourselves, so we silenced our critical selves and tried to blot out the criticism of others with alcohol or other drugs.

Some of us had our initial experiences with alcohol or other drugs because of peer pressure. We wanted to be accepted, to be one of the crowd, so we went along with our friends.

Even when recovering parents didn't start out drinking or using other drugs in order to be accepted or block out feelings of failure, chances are as the alcoholism or other drug addiction progressed, acceptance and the lack of it attained major importance in their lives. Old friends often began turning cold shoulders when behavior got out of control, and a chemically dependent person had to find a new set of friends who not only accepted but encouraged chemical abuse and the bizarre behavior that came with it. Spouses, relatives, and employers often became more critical and less accepting as drinking or other drug use affected relationships and work. The more out of control our lives became, the more difficult it was to accept ourselves.

Many alcoholics, before they reach bottom, decide they will drink only on weekends, will drink only one type of liquor, only one brand of liquor, never before noon. The inability to stick to those rules creates huge black clouds of frustration and failure hanging over them.

The more bitter failures and frustrations we've experienced in our lives, the bigger tendency we have to live through our children. Some of us try so hard to undo our mistakes by pushing our children to achieve our goals, we are blinded to the fact that they aren't us and they never can be. If we don't accept our children as individuals, we, like Ben's dad, hand them a legacy of failure.

Control. Four-year-old Brian's father is a drinking alcoholic. His mom gets Valium from three different physicians because no one doctor will prescribe enough to help her "get through the day with that lush." Most of the time his parents ignore him, concentrating on their addictions and on the ongoing war between them. However, Brian has found several extremely effective ways to get attention. His first tactic is to get a running start from across the room and butt his head into his mother's stomach. It has never failed to get her attention. Most of the time she lectures him about what an awful little boy he is and swats him on the behind, but when she feels guilty for paying so little attention to him, she takes him on her lap and hugs him.

Since his mom's reaction depends on her internal state and isn't predictable, Brian can never be sure whether his assaults are O.K. or taboo. He only is certain they are a good way to get Mom to acknowledge he is there, and so the assaults continue.

Brian's whininess and refusal to obey at bedtime cause his dad's temper to flare. When he's in a fairly mellow mood and has consumed only one or two drinks, he tells Brian he doesn't like his attitude and sends him to his room. He is also sure to enforce a prompt eight o'clock lights out policy. But when Dad's had several beers or is hung over, Brian gets sent to his room before he even opens his mouth and sometimes even when he's been playing quietly, Dad sends him to bed an hour or two early. Sometimes Dad is so drunk he simply ignores his son's whines and forgets about putting Brian to bed entirely. The boy falls asleep in front of the T.V. some time around midnight.

Even an adult would have difficulty figuring out what Brian's parents expect from him in the way of behavior! They've never defined his limits to him in a clear way he can understand. Though he's an intelligent boy, he can't possibly begin to comprehend a term like "attitude." It simply doesn't mean anything to him.

His problems with his parents go even deeper than understanding the rules he is to follow, because Brian's folks give him mixed messages about how he is to act. Sometimes it's fine to stay up as late as he wants to, yet other times he's banished to his bedroom early. A battering attack on Mom may get him a hug or a swat and he has no way of predicting which it will be ahead of time. Because, like all children, he needs limits to know what he can and cannot do, he is constantly testing his parents in an attempt to goad them into structuring his world.

At a young age Brian has learned that the world is unpredictable and that there isn't a whole lot he can do to control it or himself. Not only do the people around him seem to react to his misdeeds by whim, often they react unfairly and out of proportion to what he's done. Brian has chosen to take the risk of punishment in order to seek attention from his parents. Other children pull inside of themselves under these circumstances and try to avoid as much contact as possible with their parents.

Because Brian's mom doesn't separate her son's feelings from his actions and labels him an "awful little boy," Brian tangles up who he is with what he does. Even though he can't yet put it into words, he sees himself as an awful little boy and his need for attention as awful, too. That's what makes Mom angry most of the time, isn't it?

Children need external limits set by parents so that they can internalize those limits as adults and develop self control. They need, as well, to know that wanting attention and feeling angry or sad are valid states. Fair and consistent discipline shows children that some ways of expressing those feelings and needs are inappropriate. Good discipline includes consistent logical consequences for children's misbehavior while allowing for appropriate ways for children to express their feelings and make their needs known.

It is frightening to grow up in a world where punishment and praise are given in willy-nilly fashion, where the rules keep changing and before you have a chance to learn them, the people in charge are furious at you for breaking them. Because alcohol and other drug abusers live a life of constant ups and downs, highs and lows, it is extremely difficult for them to be consistent either in making rules for their children or in enforcing them.

Guidance. Fourteen-year-old Rhonda's mother began drinking shortly after she became promoted to a managerial position at the bank four years ago. Initially, she discovered that business lunches which consisted of gin and tonics helped ease the pressures of her new position. Later she began drinking in the evening to unwind from a rough day at the office and now she continues her alcohol consumption until she retires to bed early, "exhausted" from the demands of her work.

Rhonda, who had enjoyed a close relationship with her mom, has recently sought emotional solace in a boyfriend— a boyfriend who pressured her for sex. Uncertain about whether to give in when she doesn't feel ready, or to stand firm and possibly lose him, she had tried talking to her mother. Mom was too depressed with her own problems to listen. "Honey, I'm just not up to a heavy conversation right now," she heard. "Let's talk later, when I'm feeling better." Later never came.

Now Rhonda thinks she might be pregnant and she doesn't know who to turn to. Her boyfriend has told her that if she gets "knocked up," that's her problem. Her dad is nervous about her mother's drinking problem and about what will happen if she loses her job and the family must do without the second income. He's been staying away from the house more and more often and Rhonda suspects he may be having an affair.

Even though Rhonda is certain her mom cares about her, she is afraid to bother her overburdened and troubled parent with her problem. It just might be the straw that breaks the camel's back and causes Mom to drink even more and go off the deep end. So, terrified, Rhonda keeps her secret to herself and prays that if she really is pregnant, it won't make her mom's condition worse.

Kids of all ages need guidance. While discipline teaches them to avoid inappropriate behavior, guidance shows positive alternatives. All children are faced with choices and it is a parent's job to enable them to make *wise* choices. Often alcoholic and other drug abusing parents are so caught up in their own dilemmas and their addiction, they have little or no time to listen to a child and to offer advice and help. How can you tell another person to cope when you can't cope, yourself?

Parents guide their children not only through heart-to-heart talks, but by example as well. Over time, the relationships of chemically dependent people deteriorate and become fragmented. Kids can't look to their chemically dependent parent to teach them how to get along with other people because that parent is unable to form healthy relationships.

Seven-year-old Jack retreated to his room when his mom drank, became angry, and argued with him. Over time, he began spending more and more time alone. When he did play with other children, he picked on them, hitting and becoming verbally abusive when he didn't get his way. Once, when a child cut ahead of him in line at a museum, he leapt on the smaller boy and bit him. "You've got to stick up for your rights," he explained later. "My mom knows how to stick up for herself." He recounted a time when an elderly woman had cut in front of his mother at the supermarket and Mom had told the senior citizen to "go to hell." Certainly Jack's mother didn't advise him to hurt other people, but he had modeled his actions after hers.

Even when Jack visited his nondrinking father several states away during his summer vacations, he carried many of the lessons he'd learned in an alcoholic household with him. The day after his paternal grandmother left after a week-long visit, Jack suddenly appeared lethargic and lost his appetite. Usually coordinated, he began stumbling and his speech became slurred. When Jack's dad found the full quart bottle of mouthwash on the bathroom shelf suddenly empty, he confronted his son.

At first Jack denied that he'd drunk the mouthwash, which had a high alcohol content. Later he admitted that he often drank mouthwash when the adults weren't looking and that at home he regularly snuck beer from the refrigerator. "It makes me feel good when I'm sad," he told his father. "But I don't have to drink it. I can quit any time I want to just like my mom."

Even though a parent may preach, "Don't do as I do; do as I tell you to do," the lesson being taught is inescapable: when the going gets tough, turn to alcohol or other drugs. Certainly, most kids can see that these don't solve problems. Every day, they observe that these "solutions" only make the existing problems worse. Yet, too often, children of chemically dependent people haven't seen any alternatives for dealing with problems besides escape into drink and other drugs.

Independence. Many children who are raised in alcoholic households take on independent, adult-like roles at an early age. Karen is one of them. From the time she was six, she has comforted her younger brother, Mark, when her mom's drinking has resulted in long crying bouts and loud arguments with her husband. Because Mom began drinking shortly after Mark was born, Karen has served as "little mommy," changing diapers, fixing bottles, and watching him for nearly seven years now.

When Mom can't cook, Karen fixes meals. She is the one who cleans house and does the grocery shopping with her dad. She also listens to him unload his troubles after a long day of work at an insurance agency and commiserates with him about her mother's drinking problem. Over the years, she's slipped into the role of "little wife" and although there's been no overt sexual contact between Karen and her dad, he relates as adult to adult rather than as parent to child with her.

On the surface it looks as if Karen is extremely independent. After all, she goes through the motions of being thirteen going on forty. Yet, inside she's very insecure and has managed to make few friends at school. When something out of the ordinary happens, be it a surprise quiz in one of her classes or an unexpected change in her study schedule at home, she reacts with panic and almost compulsively throws herself into working harder. There are few occasions when she'll allow herself to have fun. When opportunities to interact with peers arise, she turns them down, afraid to risk trying anything new.

Children like Karen may appear to be extremely independent and competent, but often living in an alcoholic household means a child must take on responsibility he or she isn't ready to assume. Because there isn't a solid and secure foundation to fall back on, no safety net, these children may be very fearful of taking emotional risks.

Mark, at seven-and-a-half, is constantly in trouble at school for his babyish behavior. He is terrified of dogs, crossing streets, and still can't tie his shoes. Karen protects him from the world, and both she and her dad protect him from the "secret" of Mom's drinking.

In some families the youngest child, or a child who seems more vulnerable than the rest, may be treated as the baby like Mark is. Family members work together to protect the child from both the knowledge and the affects of a parent's chemical dependency. Sometimes, being overprotective to a child makes siblings and parents, the chemically dependent parent included, feel needed. As long as the child is dependent and can't cope, the people who protect that child are necessary parts of the family. Many times an "incompetent" and immature child masks a deteriorating marriage relationship or a parental drinking or other drug problem. As long as Mom and Dad can focus on the child's overwhelming demands to be nurtured, they aren't forced to look at the real issues at stake: relationship problems or chemical dependency.

Protection. It is a rare parent, chemically dependent or otherwise, who doesn't want to protect his or her children from physical harm. Unfortunately alcoholism and other drug addiction often prevents us from acting on our good intentions by impairing our judgment about what is best for our children. Chemically dependent parents are in a double bind as they try to keep their children safe. We may *know* that alcohol is involved in over half of all fatal traffic accidents, but we drive under the influence anyway, often with our children beside us. Since, at all costs, we can't admit to our addiction, we often place our kids in dangerous situations and pretend they're normal situations. To admit we have a drinking or other drug problem would mean we'd risk having to give it up, and we can't conceive of living without the substance we're addicted to.

Pulled in two directions at once, wanting to keep our children safe and needing our drinks or other drugs, we addicted parents often rationalize and compromise. Even though a parent may know deep inside that the physical safety of a child is *not* to be compromised, our impaired judgment prevents us from acting on that knowledge. If a parent is inebriated and needs to go somewhere with the child, it's fine to drive, the rationalization goes. "I'm a *better* driver when I've had a couple of drinks." When a single parent wants to go to a bar, sometimes an inadequate sitter seems better than none.

"The bar is only around the corner," Melissa told herself when she contemplated leaving her eight-year-old son and six-year-old daughter to care for themselves. "I'll only be gone an hour or two and they're asleep for the night. What could happen?" Any number of things could have happened. Most recovering parents can offer a silent prayer of thanks that nothing bad ever did happen to the children.

Others aren't so lucky. Within a two week period in Denver, Colorado, alcohol-related deaths of three children made headlines. A couple left their son and his friend in their car while they dropped into a party for a few minutes. The boys were asleep and the parents left the engine running so the heater would keep the children warm. Hours later they emerged from the party, drove home, and tried to awaken the boys. Both children had died from carbon monoxide poisioning.

In the second case, the drinking parent put her children in danger through abuse rather than neglect. When her six-year-old son escaped the home and told neighbors his mother was killing his baby sister, police rushed to the scene and found the two-year-old daughter dead from being battered with a toy rifle.

Most alcoholic and other drug-abusing parents do not physically abuse or neglect their children, but the incidence of family violence and neglect in homes where there are alcohol and other drug problems is higher than in other homes. Sometimes a parent becomes violent when alcohol or other drugs dissolves inhibitions. Other times the chemicals offer an "excuse" to become violent. Probation officers and social workers hear a constant litany: "I couldn't help myself; I was drinking. I couldn't help myself; I'd taken drugs."

Occasionally the chemically dependent parent doesn't commit abuse, but is incapacitated and stands by helplessly while a spouse or boyfriend harms children. The parent may be afraid to disclose the family secret of physical or sexual abuse to authorities out of fear his or her drinking or other drug problem will be discovered and the children taken away.

Faith. Faith is an elusive ingredient, one we grapple with during most of our childhood and adulthood. Some of us have a deep and abiding faith in God. Others are content with faith that the sun will come up tomorrow just as it did today. Some of us classify our belief system as religion, others call it philosophy or ethics. All of us have beliefs, faith in something, and those beliefs guide our actions.

When we were drinking or using other drugs, we had a spiritual illness. Our addiction, rather than our beliefs and values, guided our every conscious thought and action. As we began to act more and more out of sync with our personal code of ethics, we had a choice. We could scratch the beliefs we'd lived by up until that point or we could get rid of our addiction. Most of us took the path of least resistance and chose the former course of action. We stopped believing in anything except another drink or a couple more pills. Parents transmit their beliefs and values to their children. Too often, our accounts were bankrupt of faith. We had little or nothing to transmit.

One of the most important steps to recovery is regaining faith as directed in A.A.'s Second and Third Steps. [*We*] *came to believe that a Power greater than ourselves could restore us to sanity.* [*We*] *made a decision to turn our will and our lives over to the care of God* as we understood Him.[4] Regardless of what we believe our Higher Power to be, the very fact that we hold a set of positive beliefs (some call them values) enables us to live full lives.

John, who grew up in a strict fundamentalist home and is now an alcoholic, wants his kids to be good people. He talks to them loud and long about the evils of lying and punishes them when he catches them in untruths. Yet he hides bottles and lies to himself and his family about how much he drinks—and his children know it. When John is hung over, he has his wife call his workplace and say he is sick with flu.

Trustworthiness is extremely important to John. He tells his kids repeatedly that you can't trust a man if his word isn't worth the paper it's written on. Yet, most of the promises he makes to his children, he breaks. He doesn't mean to go back on his word, but something (usually a couple of six packs) gets in the way.

Although he sends his children to church, he's ashamed to go himself. After he's had several beers, he criticizes God for making his life so miserable. John's kids are being raised in a moral vacuum. They sit in the eye of the hurricane while all sorts of contradictory words and actions swirl around them. It is extremely difficult for them to make sense of the world or to have faith in anything.

---

[4] Ibid.

What we believe in *is* very important, but it's a personal matter. Wars that changed the course of history have been fought over differences in faith. There are over a thousand religious denominations in the U.S. alone—all exist because of sometimes minute, sometimes huge, differences in faith. Frequently, recovering alcoholics get stuck on the issue of faith and spend hours debating the concept of a Higher Power. Should your Higher Power be a God in the traditional Hebrew or Christian sense or a more philosophical concept like Truth or a Prime Cause? That decision is up to *you.*

We are directed in A.A.'s Eleventh Step to develop an active relationship with our personal Higher Power. [*We*] *Sought through prayer and meditation to improve our conscious contact with God as we understood Him, praying only for knowledge of His will for us and the power to carry that out.*[5] The result is a spiritual awakening, one which enables us to carry the message to other alcoholics and helps us to practice A.A. principles in all our affairs—including our relationships with our children.

In the meantime, our children need our guidance in order to learn regard for qualities like kindness, justice, courage, generosity, and honesty. Without values and beliefs, children grow up empty and confused. They have no solid inner core to rely on in times of trouble, and they have no set of standards to help them make decisions. The problem with a parent's spiritual illness is that it is highly contageous. Even though some of us must wrestle with the concept of the Higher Power, the struggle is one we need to go through if we and our children are going to make a successful recovery.

Love, security, acceptance, control, guidance, independence, protection, and faith. You've taken inventory now and have a good idea of which supplies you're low on and

---

[5] Ibid.

which you have in abundance. Because you've finished the painful job of making an assessment, you have a list of the things your children need for the journey ahead, and some idea of what you can do to fill those needs. You've taken another step, a big one. You're making progress!

THREE

How Our Children Learned to Cope

Children are resilient and their instinct is for survival. In homes where few or only some of their emotional needs are met, they survive by adapting. We've seen some instances of how children may not be getting their needs filled when they live in a chemically dependent home. Now it's time to explore some of the coping strategies children of chemically dependent parents sometimes use in order to minimize the impact of that parent's alcohol or other drug addiction on their lives.

Not all kids acquire the same coping skills for life's stresses, just as we adults vary in the way we handle continuing problems. Some of us withdraw and try not to think about the troublesome parts of our lives which we can't change. We learn to keep a very low profile. Others, when faced with stressful work or marriage situations, seek out other areas in which we can excel. We find hobbies or pursuits which enable us to feel good about ourselves. A few of us hold in anger about bad situations we can't seem to change, and then our anger spills over in inappropriate ways. Or we might develop some sort of defense mechanism to keep the pain at bay. My husband seeks refuge in long naps when his life becomes troubled. I, on the other hand, stay up nights worrying. Everyone has his or her own way of reacting to stress.

Children who live in a chemically dependent home are subjected to a good deal of stress. Often, they cannot predict how a chemically dependent parent will act. Will Mom show up drunk at the school play and embarrass us? Will she show up at all? Is Dad coming home from work tonight? If he does, will he be angry and spend the night yelling at us? Even occasions like dinnertime, and what started out to be a lazy Sunday afternoon around the house, can explode into ugly and frightening scenes. If they are to protect themselves, most kids find ways to handle this uncertainty. Like adults, some of them hit on healthier, more productive ways to handle stress than others.

Some of the negative effects living with an alcoholic parent or parents can cause center on problems in school. A few, but not all, children of alcoholics throw tantrums in school and get into trouble with adult authority figures such as teachers and playground supervisors. Children of alcoholics may be absent from school often and have trouble with their grades. When parental chemical abuse stops, kids may have an easier time studying and completing homework. They may be able to get a decent night's sleep and don't have to stay home to care for an incapacitated parent. Sometimes, though, school problems don't just disappear when the parent's drinking ceases, and then it's important to look into this issue more deeply.

Some research has discovered emotional problems which show up in some kids from alcoholic homes. Again, some, but not all children of alcoholics may experience difficulty forming and maintaining relationships with family and peers, they may suffer from low self-esteem and have a very hard time accepting and talking about their anger and hostility.

Reality! What reality?

A big problem a child may face when he or she grows up in a home where drinking or other drugs has been a controlling factor for a long time is the inability to know what is real and what is not. Caught up in the denial system, the child sees one thing to be true, but hears that it isn't. "I'm not drunk; this is grape-juice!" "Your dad didn't park the car on the front lawn. You must be hearing things." When a child is warned not to believe what he or she sees, a major conflict is created. Some children of alcoholics have trouble learning what is real and what is not when a parent stops drinking and the family unhooks from the denial process.

When seven-year-old Jack visits his nondrinking dad, he is frequently caught "red-handed" taking his stepbrother's toys and destroying them. Even when discovered in the act he vehemently denies any connection to the broken toys. He often watches his stepmother and his father observing his misbehaviors, but that only seems to increase his innocent protests. It is difficult for Jack's other family to realize that denial is Jack's way of coping with unpleasantness, that he isn't a bald-faced liar. He's learned from his alcoholic mom that reality is what you make it; truth is what serves him at the moment. Scolding him for being a liar only puts bigger dents in his self-concept than are already there. Many times Jack responds with overtly hostile actions and even bigger "whoppers" to deny them.

It can be very hard for a recovering parent to deal with a child's inability to tell truth from falsehood. Recovering parents who haven't fully let go of denial mechanisms may recognize them in their kids, but decide to go along with it rather than taking the more difficult course of reinforcing reality to the child. Understand that, in all probability, kids who constantly tell tall tales and distort the truth aren't doing it to spite you. They *do* need your calm help in learning to accept reality and to stop hiding behind illusion and denial. In some cases they need professional help.

It should be noted here that researchers find a number of children with home lives disrupted by chemically dependent or even mentally ill parents, who don't seem to be negatively affected at all by their parents' problems. The technical term for these kids is "competent" or "invulnerable." How do they manage to live in a less than enviable home and come out well adjusted? Some are resilient and adapt well to the circumstances around them. Researchers have found that a number of these children have effective coping skills. They are effective in play, work, love, self-esteem, self-discipline, and can think abstractly. These kids make sense of the world around them and act on it. In short, they have a good sense of reality and somehow have managed to avoid being trapped in denial.

The degree of a parent's alcoholism is only *moderately* related to the degree of disturbance in his or her children, researchers tell us. Sometimes alcoholism or other drug abuse covers other problems a parent may have. In such circumstances a severely troubled parent in the early stages of chemical dependency might have a more negative impact on children than a parent in the middle or late stages of the disease who doesn't have problems unrelated to the addiction.

The idea that substance-abusing moms have greater negative impact on their children's lives than do alcoholic or substance-abusing dads hasn't been adequately researched. Some studies seem to show maternal alcoholism more profoundly affects children, but others contradict those findings. Generalizations may be tempting, but they aren't always valid!

Children *don't* generally sit up nights in their rooms, mapping out survival strategy. Most of the time they discover ways to handle stress, ways to meet their needs, by a trial and error basis. When something works, a child remembers and tries it again. Used often enough, a stress survival tactic can become second nature.

If Dad rushes past five-year-old David when he comes home from work, and goes straight for the bottle instead,

David might throw a tantrum out of anger. Immediately, Dad turns his attention to his son. Whether he punishes him or comforts him, he's telling David, "When you do this, you come first in my life. I pay attention to you." After the incident is repeated several times, David knows, without any conscious thought or planning, that temper tantrums work to meet his needs and reduce the stress of being rejected by his father. He's learned a way to cope.

Five-year-old Jonathan, under the same set of circumstances, might hit on the idea of standing on his head and acting silly, to cheer Dad up and win him over through humor. Gloria, the same age, could offer to help fix Daddy's drink for him and engage him in an "adult" conversation.

The particular set of coping strategies a child works out through trial and error depends on a number of factors. In the first place, each child has a different personality. The behaviors that may work for energetic and live-wire Mary aren't the same as those which shy and introverted George down the street will find useful.

As we discussed earlier, not all chemically dependent parents are alike either. The child of a binge-drinking father who disappears for a couple of days every two or three months is faced with a different situation and stress than the child whose mom or dad passes out every night on the sofa after vomiting on the living room floor. A kid whose parent takes drugs and withdraws faces a different set of challenges than a kid whose parent drinks and becomes aggressive and verbally or physically abusive.

Chemically dependent families vary a great deal in their stability. Some families are nearly constantly chaotic and the children in them are subjected to a number of risk factors. Physical and sexual abuse, divorce, death in the family, unemployment, loud arguments, the confining of a parent to a jail or a mental hospital, all might be linked to the chemical abuse, but they pile more stress on children than the fact of chemical dependency alone. Sometimes the nondrinking parent can help children deal with stress, but in other homes that parent is too preoccupied with the disease to be of much support.

Finally, even within the same family, siblings may hit on different survival strategies. Some children may have known the parent before the onset of chemical dependency and grieve the loss of the "good old days." Younger kids might only have seen that same parent in the clutches of chemical abuse and simply accept Mommy as stumbling, having slurred speech and a quick temper. They never knew her to be otherwise.

Children's ages also can determine just which coping behaviors they have available to them. A two-year-old can't very well escape from home into the outside world of friends and school. Neither can a sixteen-year-old easily revert to soiling herself or wetting the bed at night.

There's nothing wrong with coping! But our kids' survival strategies which they have developed during our drinking days may get them into trouble when they use them inappropriately. It's a crazy world out there, but we chemically dependent people are still in the minority. The rest of the world doesn't necessarily understand how well denial works for a child with an alcoholic parent. Sometimes our children have learned their "survival lessons" so well that they use them unselectively. They may carry them to school and into relationships with friends and use their survival skills so often it seems as if they've "become" those survival skills.

After a while, David may have tantrums in the presence of Mom and then at school when his teacher ignores him in order to pay attention to another child. Unless someone intervenes and helps David stop having tantrums, pointing out alternatives which work as well or better, he might continue the tantrums right through adolescence. Of course, he would need to modify them a bit over time, but if rage and destructiveness in the form of vandalism kept working for him, he'd have little reason to give the tactic up, especially if he saw no other way to meet his needs.

New ways for old

Sometimes our children cling to the old ways of getting by after we've stopped drinking or abusing other drugs. Those coping styles can feel maddenly blatant or irritatingly subtle to us. Nine-year-old Jennifer found she could effectively escape the turmoil she felt in the pit of her stomach by watching T.V. when her single mom would regularly drink to unconsciousness. By two o'clock on Sunday she had memorized the week's T.V. listing section in the paper and had decided on exactly the shows she wanted to watch every night. She even ate her dinner in front of the set.

This was fine as long as Mom drank. Jennifer was "no trouble at all," a quiet, model child. Once Mom attained sobriety, she saw that Jennifer had no friends and no interests beyond the flickering screen. She resolved to establish a new relationship with her daughter and made plans for outings the two of them could enjoy together. She expected her daughter to be pleased, but instead Jenny cried when she had to miss one of her shows whether it was for a quiet mother-daughter talk or a Saturday shopping trip downtown complete with lunch at a hamburger stand. Mom began asking for Jennifer's input, but heard only, "I'd like to stay home and watch the special on this afternoon."

Feeling totally defeated, Jennifer's mother complained, "Sometimes I think she'd rather I was still drinking so I'd leave her alone. I get mad at her passivity and I want to shake her. Then I get mad at myself and feel depressed and guilty because I pushed her away so much in the past. Why can't she see she doesn't have to escape into television anymore?"

Because she's Jennifer and not Jennifer's mom! Our kids

can be ecstatic about the fact that we've put the plug in the jug. Their joy, however, doesn't automatically equip them with the new tool kit they need in order to relate to us as sober parents today. Their resistance to the changes we're making in our lives right now doesn't make it any easier for us. Some days it is very difficult to maintain equilibrium when children seem to be totally ignoring the fact of our sobriety and, in fact, seem to be trying to draw us back into the old, alcoholic patterns of interacting. If you refuse to go back to the old ways and resist going on a "dry drunk," eventually change will come for your children.

Remember the agonizing decision-making process you went through when you finally decided to give up drinking or drugs? Chances are it was a long and arduous decision to come to. For a while you may have wavered. You decided to prove to yourself you could do it by only drinking with friends instead of alone, only drinking at bars instead of home, only drinking wine instead of hard liquor. Even though you were changing internally, coming face to face with the monster of addiction, you still may have kept right on drinking. You needed to make your decision and come to your own realizations in your own time. They were *your* decisions, *your* realizations, no one else's.

Most of us have a head start on our kids when it comes to adjusting to our sobriety. They will take the risks of relating to us and to the world around them in new, more productive ways, when *they* feel comfortable with the risk-taking. Sometimes it may seem as if they still treat you like a falling-down drunk or a hopelessly stoned druggie— they may not know how to act as if you aren't. With some conscious effort on your part, you can help them explore new ways of handling life and reacting to anxiety. And you can find ways of doing this that don't involve badgering, cajoling, or lecturing which tend to make kids dig in their heels even more firmly. You can also focus on your own recovery process. Those old patterns of relating aren't set in cement, even though early on it may seem that way. The stronger you become in your newfound sobriety, the weaker those old ways will become.

How do they cope?

There are a number of ways children learn to cope with alcoholism or other drug addiction in the home. As we'll see, under certain circumstances these ways of adapting can be very positive. There should be no real cause for panic if you happen to recognize your children's coping methods in the sections below. You might even see a bit of yourself as you read. There *is* cause for concern when kids use one or two coping methods excessively or inappropriately. (Your straight "A" scholar has no interests except studying and has set even higher goals for herself—if she doesn't win a full scholarship to Harvard she'll never come out of her room again! Your junior Rodney Dangerfield tells jokes constantly and never seems to get serious, even if the situation demands it—when the dog got run over, he did a dead dog imitation!)

The survival strategies detailed below aren't exclusive to children of chemically dependent people. My parents were only occasional, moderate drinkers, and I still struggle with my own perfectionism, which at times borders on the ridiculous. Who in her right mind would bake the same cake three times for the P.T.A. bake sale to get it exactly, gorgeously like the picture in *Good Housekeeping?* Neither is the list all-inclusive. Kids are creative, and they're always coming up with something new.

It's important to keep in mind as you read, that often popular methods of classifying children of alcoholics, although they may be helpful, tend to be simplistic. Not all children are the same, not all alcoholics are the same, not all families are the same. There's no magic formula into which you can plug one or two variables such as birth order or eye color and come up with an instant and accurate diagnosis for your children.

The object isn't to make a diagnosis at all, but to figure out whether or not your children's coping skills fit their new situation—life with a recovering parent rather than a drunken or drugged one.

Perfectionism. Some kids with an alcoholic parent or parents seem to be saying, "If I do the best I can and don't do anything wrong, then everything's going to be O.K." Many times, striving to be perfect, whether it's in the classroom, on the football field, or in social areas, begins as a way a child can feel good about him- or herself. It's also a very effective way to get attention and approval from a parent who is turning more and more to drink or other drugs. Some kids perceive their parents' addiction as their fault, and they work hard to undo the substance abuse by getting higher grades, becoming president of the student body, or the bounciest cheerleader on the squad. The magical thinking goes that once they get good enough, their drinking or other drug using parent will no longer need their habit.

Unfortunately, no matter what a kid does, a parent who is addicted isn't going to quit. The cause of the addiction has nothing to do with the child; it lies solely within the parent. Our children may only see that they've failed in their efforts to please us. Some of them give up. Others boost their efforts over and over again until they resemble junior workaholics. While striving toward goals is a very positive way for a child or an adult to behave, sometimes the goals become either unrealistically high or secondary to the very process of trying to achieve them. In George Santayana's words: "Fanaticism consists in redoubling your effort when you have forgotten your aim."

Seven-year-old Mary, a gifted student, is her teacher's favorite. When she's assigned to do a paragraph report, she invariably turns in several pages of work complete with drawings. Often she volunteers to stay after school and clean the blackboards or tidy up the room. Whenever she turns in a flawed assignment, she redoes the entire thing the next day even though it isn't required. Even the slightest criticism can provoke tears. In class discussions, her hand is always raised and she seems distressed and hurt if she isn't called on.

At home Mary washes and dries all her own clothing, a task her alcoholic mother is seldom up to doing. Mary takes hours insuring that her school clothes are spotless and she refuses to wear anything if it is even slightly wrinkled. Her room is always neat and she gets very upset if something is out of place. She takes piano lessons, and though her music teacher praises her for her astounding progress, Mary only sees her own mistakes and pushes herself harder. Lately she's begun making lists of all the tasks she hopes to accomplish both at school and at home, including perfect playing of even the piano pieces she's never played before. When she fails to cross an item off her list, she punishes herself by skipping desert at dinner.

Because Mary is such an exemplary child, her parents and her teacher have difficulty seeing that her superkid routine covers a lot of pain. The fact that she doesn't play and never seems to relax is hidden behind her accomplishments. She's rewarded for her singleminded drive toward absolute perfection by good grades and lavish praise from her piano teacher, her classroom teacher, and her father. Even Mom is obviously proud of her superstar daughter.

There are several things a recovering parent can do to help a child unhook from the burden of perfectionism. If you see that your child has too much invested in accomplishments, you can make a special effort to give him or her attention at the times he or she isn't locked into striving. By the same token, if you've focused a great deal of attention in the past on accomplishments, you might want to start selectively ignoring some of the child's achievements and redirecting the conversation to other topics which aren't achievement-oriented. "I like you for who you are, not only for what you do," is the message you need to get across, both in words and actions. Children like Mary need to know it isn't the end of the world if they make a mistake; you'll still love them.

Becoming indispensible. As alcoholism or other drug addiction progresses, parents find it more and more difficult to fulfill their roles. Dishes don't get done, absence excuses for school don't get signed. An enterprising child doesn't need to be a genius to find tasks which need to be done and quietly set about doing them. Because it's every parent's dream to have the kids' rooms picked up and the trash taken out without having to nag about it, we rarely notice when our kids have taken on too much responsibility in an attempt to become an indispensible part of our lives.

In fact, when our children have learned how to cover our alcoholism and other drug addiction from the outside world, and when they protect us from the consequences of our addiction, they *do* become indispensible to us because they make it easier for us to drink or to take other drugs. We sense that without their caretaking, we'd have to face our problem head on and possibly give up the substances we're abusing.

After Joanna's mom and dad had the argument about how dinner was sometimes late, sometimes burned, and never good and Mom set out still-frozen macaroni and cheese dinners one night, Joanna knew implicitly what to do. She began reading cookbooks and making dinner, but entering into an agreement with Mom that they'd pretend *she* was still cooking. The thirteen-year-old daughter carefully hid the evidence of her mom's drinking when she came home from school, carrying Mom's empties down the alley to the trash can three houses down.

When a teacher called and requested a conference with

Mom about Joanna's little brother, she explained her mother had a lingering illness, but that *she* would be glad to speak with the teacher in her place. She began taking the responsibility of making sure her siblings were well dressed and clean for school. She helped them with their homework and began doing the baking for P.T.A. bake sales and a younger sister's Girl Scout meetings.

The teenager was such a positive force in her family that, more and more, her parents and brothers and sisters came to depend on her. It became Joanna whom they turned to for leadership and direction when Mom had too much to drink and Dad was unavailable, which seemed more and more of the time. Joanna was the one who decided to try and fix the old washing machine rather than buy a new one. In time she became the head of the family, doing the shopping and the mending, the cleaning and the parenting.

She was so good at it that everyone seemed to forget she was still a kid and ought to be out having fun with others her own age. "She's so serious and mature," her dad often commented. "Someday she'll make some man a perfect wife." But his daughter had already assumed the role of wife without having had time to explore other roles or to define herself outside of her function in her family. She'd gone from childhood to adulthood without an adolescence.

Recovering parents who notice that their children seem to have become too responsible and independent need to begin paying attention to their kids' accomplishments outside the home and praising them for those. Many times these little adults have been too busy to form friendships with peers, and they may look at other kids their own age as being immature and frivolous. It's too much to ask to insist that an overly responsible child suddenly become a giddy adolescent. Recovering parents can, however, begin assuming the functions and jobs they couldn't perform when they weren't sober. They can also acknowledge that

61

they understand it *is* difficult for a child to suddenly feel somewhat useless at home and out of his or her element with friends. Sometimes encouragement is enough to help a child begin living as a child again. Other times, a recovering parent may need to help set up situations for peer interaction, like offering to have a child's friend for an overnight visit, or volunteering to drive a group of kids to the video arcade or a movie.

Remaining firm in your position as a competent adult who can and will resume your role in the family is very important. When you have a bad day, it is tempting to allow an overly responsible child to take over your responsibilities again. Even though all children should have some tasks to accomplish around the house, you do your child and yourself a great disservice when you let him or her fill your shoes.

Peacemaking. According to the Sermon on the Mount, peacemakers are blessed. Indeed, a child who can oil the troubled waters, soothe ruffled feathers, and make peace between the sometimes warring factions in a chemically dependent household, is a valuable child. Some children seem to follow after an alcohol or other drug-addicted parent, picking up the emotional pieces and calming family members whose feelings have been hurt. "Mom didn't mean to yell at you; she's just tired." The role of peacemaker becomes damaging to a child when that child can no longer think about his or her own needs and, instead, begins to live by the rule of appeasement at all costs.

When fourteen-year-old Bill's dad would come home drunk after his thrice weekly evenings out with the boys, he'd frequently be threatening and abusive to Bill's mom and his younger brothers and sisters. Because Bill was a natural diplomat, calm and gentle, mature beyond his years, he was quickly cast into the role of Dad's keeper. He was the one who rationally talked his father out of his tempers and got him into bed. He also calmed down the rest of the family and carefully steered them out of Dad's way. It was Bill who kept the social service workers away from the door and everybody knew it, including Dad. Bill was admired for his peacemaking abilities and rewarded for them by the secure knowledge that he was needed. He was someone his family, his father, too, couldn't do without.

Acutely attuned to everyone else's needs, Bill (and his family) were unaware of his own. He rarely allowed himself to feel anger and disappointment even with friends because he was too busy handling others' negative feelings. He learned to anticipate the emotional needs of others and to meet them before they even asked. Kids like Bill are in danger of becoming "yes men and women," subverting their needs to the needs and demands of family, friends, and teachers. Afraid of making waves or rocking the boat, they are careful to express only opinions others will agree with and to please others even at their own expense.

Children who have become appeasers and pleasers need to be reassured that the anger and displeasure of other people won't make the sky fall in on them. It is possible to have a difference of opinion with another person and still care about them. Recovering parents can encourage their peacemaking children to develop and express opinions of their own, opinions which may differ from those of parents. Foster a climate in which children can be free to think and act on their own needs and help show them the difference between taking the needs of others into consideration and living one's life through others. Older children might benefit from an assertiveness training class offered through school, church, or a social service agency.

Distracting. Comic relief is a very effective tension reliever. One of the reasons Shakespeare's tragedies work is because when the tension and suspense build to almost unbearable levels, comic characters are introduced and walk across the stage telling jokes and making puns. Some kids decide that laughter is the best medicine and they seem to go about turning life into a comedy routine. Most parents, when tired of hearing the same third grade joke for the seventh time in an evening, wind up moaning, "enough is enough," and set parameters for their kids. Sometimes a witty sense of humor is necessary and appropriate, but at other times a joke or silliness just isn't the appropriate response.

Six-year-old Reuben relates to the world through the guise of a clown. In his first grade classroom he pulls the chair out from behind other children and constantly makes faces behind the teacher's back. His mother and his alcoholic dad rarely take their son out in public any more. While Mom is filling out her deposit slip at the bank, Reuben gets down on all fours beneath the counter and barks like a dog, threatening to bite other bank patron's ankles. He's been known to dump a full milkshake container over on himself at the local fast-food restaurant, simply to break up the other diners. Often he gives an encore performance with loud burping.

Reuben's problem is that he just can't stop. After five such "accidents" while the family was eating out, they began dining at home. More and more often his mom leaves him with a neighbor when she has to run errands. She even tries to avoid taking her son along when she shops for clothes for him because Reuben invariably makes a game out of it, hiding in the dressing rooms. Now his welcome at the babysitter's is wearing thin. Reuben stands in the woman's back yard when parents arrive, shakes up his apple juice or pop so that it has a head of foam like Dad's beer and regales neighbors to an imitation of the woman—drunk, a condition she's never experienced.

Because Reuben is "cute" and puckish with his cherubic face and large, dark eyes, people often find him irresistible. Sometimes his humor is on target and family members, as well as teachers and the lady who watches him, find themselves laughing. When Reuben "accidentally" spills his drink in a restaurant, other customers smile and shake their heads. He's so caught up in their first reactions, he fails to see or care about the disgust registered on their faces when he launches into his sound effects.

Underneath their comedy routine, kids like Reuben are often fearful and depressed. They are running away from the issues of chemical dependency in their homes and frequently can't communicate in any other way besides their facade of humor. Recovering parents need to observe their "laugh-a-minute" youngsters and discover whether the humor is appropriate or if these kids seem to compulsively hunger for laughter, attention, and approval. It may be time to have your family comic sit down for *short*, serious talks, and to insist upon eye contact during those conversations.

By all means, laugh when your Reuben tells an appropriate joke, but don't when the humor is overdone or inappropriate. Sometimes family comics elude responsibility not only for their feelings, but for jobs within the family as well. You'd hardly ask the family fool to do such a complicated task as wash the clothes—they might dye all the clothes purple just for the fun of it! It's time to insist that children like this start to take on some responsibility and to begin rewarding and praising them for that instead of focusing entirely on the humor. Kids like Reuben need to find other ways to feel good about themselves besides their ability to make people laugh.

Finally, because the compulsive comedy often masks a real terror of getting angry or showing any feelings like sadness, jealousy, or disgust, you'll need to let your child know it's O.K. to express negative feelings. It isn't the end of the world when people stop belly laughing. You can do this by allowing yourself to get angry when the child starts "bouncing off the walls" and acting like all of the Three Stooges rolled into one. Anger is an appropriate response when you're on the phone and Jimmy or Nora begins banging his or her head against the wall and then staggering and writhing on the floor in order to get your attention.

After you've expressed your anger, you can talk about it calmly with the child and then make up. Often when a comic who hasn't learned how to express emotions in other ways, *sees* appropriate emotional expression and learns first-hand that there is little to fear from it, it can be enough impetus to try something other than a joke when the situation demands it.

Rebelling. It's a rare parent who hasn't heard, "No! I *won't* clean my room!" or "I hate you!" In fact, as our children grow older, they invariably seem to perceive us as being out of touch with what's going on with the world. We like the wrong kind of music. We, who haven't changed the way we dress in years, suddenly dress "funny." Our political beliefs are antiquated and our values predate the Dark Ages. Kids do reach a certain stage where they must define themselves in terms of themselves if they are to become their own adults instead of our perpetual children. Rebellion is a natural and gradual process of growing up, and usually it's a healthy process.

It isn't healthy when children's rebelliousness and acting out endangers themselves or others. When a child's home life seems intolerable, rebellion can be speeded up and intensified. It may be too painful for a child, even a young child, to identify with a chemically dependent parent, and "I don't want any part of you. I don't want to be like you at all!" can be the response.

Other kids act out excessively because they carry around a good deal of anger. There's a lot to be angry about in a home where a parent is addicted. Promises get broken right along with the dishes and the furniture. Children become embarrassed in front of their peers. They feel uncomfortable and sometimes unwanted. Instead of asking the sometimes futile question, "How can you do this to me?" a child may act it out.

Perhaps the family's attention is so focused on the chemical dependency that there is little or none left for the child. Becoming tough and disruptive draws the attention back to the child or teenager.

Sarah, whose parents had always considered her a bit too strong willed and stubborn to their liking, took up with a rough bunch of friends in sixth grade. She began wearing too much make-up, tight clothing, and staying out all night. By the time she was in seventh grade, she'd frequently arrive home with beer on her breath, obviously inebriated. When Sarah's sedative-addicted mother drew the line and refused to give Sarah any more allowance so as not to subsidize her daughter's new lifestyle, Sarah simply began stealing money from her mom's purse, first five dollars at a time, then ten and twenty dollar bills.

During the arguments which ensued after the thefts were discovered, nobody stopped to question why Sarah's mother routinely left her pocketbook lying around with large sums of money in it. Sarah's dad would yell and threaten to send her to reform school, forgetting temporarily that the primary family problem was his wife's drug dependency. Sarah's mom would cry and withdraw, agonizing at how much her daughter had disappointed her. Brothers and sisters smugly patted themselves on the back for being good kids, not a bit like their errant sister. In the midst of the turmoil, Sarah was helping everyone to evade the reality of Mom's problem.

Recovering parents need to look past the behavior of their overly rebellious children who have the ability to try the patience of saints, and see the children themselves. Getting extremely angry, blaming and feeling defensive and resentful, hooks recovering parents right back into the old script with these kids. Learn to calmly set limits, make those limits known to the child, and enforce logical and reasonable consequences when those bounds are overstepped.

When an acting-out child blames you or others for "making" them misbehave, remind them that they are in control of their actions and they are the ones who choose to ignore or disobey the family rules you've set down. On the more positive side, notice the times your rebellious child does handle responsibility well, is courteous and acts in a mature, controlled fashion. Praise and reward the child at those times.

Finally, remember to take care of yourself and not to take all the acting out personally as a sign of your incompetence as a parent. When children act like little hellions it is easy to feel helpless and a failure as a parent. It becomes a simple matter to give up, and extremely tempting to insulate yourself from their behavior through alcohol or other drugs again. Step back, take a deep breath, and plan on doing some things for yourself: an A.A. meeting, a quiet walk in the park, a conversation with a friend. By making the struggle with rebellious offspring a life-or-death one with the power to make or break our sobriety, we give our kids more power than they deserve or can handle.

Withdrawing. Knowing when to shrug our shoulders and walk away from a problem we can't possibly solve is a thing many adults could stand to learn. A Zen-like acceptance of life and the ability to shut out distraction are extremely useful. Sometimes, though, children of chemically dependent parents carry this shutting-down process too far because a low profile approach to life is a strategy which works well in many homes where alcoholism or other drug addiction is present. "If my dad can't find me, he can't hassle me," explains a teenage boy. "And even when he does find me, I always have my headphones on. I just shut him out and he can't get to me."

When Ronald received a computer for his thirteenth birthday it was the answer to his prayers. Lately, his advertising account executive dad had begun drinking more and more and becoming more and more distant from his son. When Dad did speak to Ronald these days, he always seemed to criticize him. Ron's mom began threatening divorce, and his older sister had run away from home twice in the last year. It seemed as if the boy's world was crashing around his ears.

He only felt safe in the darkness of his room while he programmed and tinkered with his computer. He saved money for a modem and began "talking" on computer bulletin boards for hours at a time. He no longer had time for the one best friend he'd had since elementary school, so he dropped him. He began eating all his meals in his room and stopped speaking to family members. He had his computer and that was all he needed.

"He's a regular computer genius!" Dad would exclaim. Mom, having read about computer hackers, made a few weak threats about selling the computer or tossing it in the garbage, but she was too caught up in making her divorce decision and coping with Ron's sister to go any further than threats. Actually, it was better for everyone involved if Ron just kept a low profile and stayed out of their way.

Whether they choose music, daydreaming, television, computers, or any number of other things to occupy their time and attention, children who withdraw need to be given opportunities to begin interacting with their families and the rest of the human race. They *don't* need to be stripped of their all-consuming interest.

Some recovering parents feel a need to remake their withdrawn youngsters into social butterflies overnight. They push, they prod, and in the end they wind up pushing and prodding these shy and introverted kids further into their shells. Engage your withdrawer in conversations about his or her personal interests, set up situations where the child can gradually form relationships with one or two other people. Let the child slowly test the waters. Don't ignore your withdrawn child, but don't play the role of full-time social director either.

* * *

Does it mean your children are "sick" if they exhibit any of these coping behaviors? The answer to that one is a definite NO! Some kids, when under chronic stress, whether it comes from living with a chemically dependent parent or even the more common stresses of moving to a new city, adjusting to a changing adolescent body, or living through parents' divorce, learn to rely on one way of dealing with the world. They either don't learn or ignore other approaches to problem solving.

When the going gets rough, remember that reliable kids often grow up to be the pillars of society. Super achievers become sports stars and Nobel Prize winners. Turn on the T.V. and you'll see famous comedians who help us laugh at our human frailties. Rebels often become society's reformers. They push the rest of us toward change. Withdrawers may be spacing out, but solitude and contemplation also happens to be a requisite for philosphers and theoreticians. Think of your kids, not as needing complete personality reformation, but as perhaps having too much of a good thing.

When our kids haven't seen other ways to cope besides the ones they tend to overuse, it's up to us as recovering parents to show them their options so they will have choices about how to react in any given situation. We can provide a secure safety net and encourage them to try out new behaviors.

The personal growth issues they face now closely resemble our own. We tried to cope by hitting the bottle or downing a few pills. After a while, we ignored other, more appropriate, ways of dealing with life. Our substance became our first choice when handling reality, and then it became our *only* choice. Today we're striking out in new directions, exploring different ways of handling life's stresses.

Now that we're beginning to take emotional risks, learning to live our lives sober, we rely on the safety net of A.A. and the understanding friends we've met there.

Our children need to know they can rely on the advice and reassurance we can provide them as their safety net.

Without some type of moral support and encouragement, it would be difficult to try out *our* new lifestyle. All of us need to know that somebody cares. Somehow, the unknown around the next bend in the road to recovery isn't as frightening when we have traveling companions we can rely on.

Learning to think and live like a sober person doesn't come overnight for us. Learning to think and live like children of sober, nonaddicted parents won't come overnight for our children, but it will come—with our help, encouragement, and support.

FOUR

The Sobering Reality

I still remember vividly the day I heard those three words which changed my life: "You're an alcoholic!" It was summer in Phoenix and so hot the sidewalks shimmered with mirages. My son, Dylan, was spending the weekend with his dad, my ex, and I was alone. I'd never felt more alone in my life! I trudged home from the counselor's office after having called A.A. and promising to go to a meeting that very night. Promptly I crawled into bed, pulled the covers over my head, and shivered so much that my teeth chattered. How could I ever leave my burrow of quilts and face the world again?

But I was a parent and I *had* to face the world in the form of my child. The next day he slammed the front door, bounded into the house and immediately demanded I fix him dinner. Because I didn't opt for detox or some other form of inpatient treatment, I was instantly on call. No matter how much I wanted to, I couldn't stay in bed.

My ex had been an enabler throughout my drinking days and was still enabling a year after the divorce, presenting me with bottles of wine, bar recommendations, and even a fancy new corkscrew. He had too much invested in his ability to silence and control me with the declaration, "You're nothing but a damned drunk," to easily give up that power. Then, I had no health insurance. Requesting a temporary vacation from parenting wasn't an option for me.

"I want my dinner now!" Dylan's face screwed into a ferocious mask of anger, and his four-year-old voice was shrill.

My first impulse was anger. He had no right to be so demanding. After all, I was still shaky and suffering from alcohol deprivation. Couldn't he see? Didn't he know?

But he *couldn't* see and he *didn't* know. He was four years old and very hungry. He'd learned not to ask me politely for things because when I'd been drinking, soft spoken requests simply didn't register with me. He was coping with Mom in the way he knew worked best—ordering her around in a loud voice. Unfortunately, in my current state, any sound above a whisper was enough to make me feel like jumping out of my skin. He didn't *know* I'd stopped drinking and even when I told him, it didn't mean much to him; he was too young to comprehend what was happening. He had no way of getting into my shoes and knowing what I felt. Dylan was a four-year-old who needed a mother, and he couldn't help it that I felt like a *three*-year-old who needed her mother even worse than he did.

One step at a time I walked into the kitchen and prepared something simple—peanut butter and jelly sandwiches. We ate them. Dylan chattered on and on about his weekend and I pretended to listen, but was too absorbed in my own internal turmoil to carry it off. I needed time alone to think and then to organize those scattered thoughts. I had to read my A.A. literature and draw strength from somewhere. Mainly I had to keep myself from taking a drink. It would have been so easy to take Dylan and drive down to the corner liquor store. But I couldn't do that, not tonight, not any night. . . .

"You look tired. I think maybe you should go to bed early," I suggested as I had many nights when I'd been drinking. Pouting, he went off to bed without so much as a goodnight hug or kiss or even a backward glance.

So much had changed. So much had remained the same. I'd admitted my alcoholism, stopped drinking for a total of thirty-two hours and twenty-seven minutes, suffered through what seemed like an endless A.A. meeting and, from Dylan's viewpoint, not a single thing was different.

I was distracted. True, my stupor wasn't caused by alcohol now but from the lack of it, but I was still in a fog. I couldn't concentrate except to sink into maudlin thoughts about drinking.

I was irritable. By now I didn't have a hangover any longer, but I was used to wrapping myself in an insulating alcohol-induced haze. It was as if someone had suddenly turned on all the lights and cranked up the volume several decibels higher than usual.

I was self-absorbed. I had to think of my own needs and meet them as best I could. I'd substituted focusing on getting that next drink for focusing and *not* getting it or pouring it or drinking it.

For Dylan the only thing which had changed was that Mom didn't have a glass in her hand. "You were even grouchier when you first quit than you were before," he remembers, and he is right.

I'd stopped drinking which was an enormous step, but I still acted, felt, and thought like a drinking alcoholic. There was absolutely no reason for Dylan to change his ways of coping with me. His booming, demanding voice, his pouting, and his manipulation irritated me to no end, but they still worked, and he justifiably continued using them.

Even when I began getting a handle on my life and slowly began acting, feeling, and thinking like a sober parent, the ways Dylan and I related to one another didn't immediately change. For a time, it seemed as if his voice had become louder and even more insistent. His demands escalated. Confused and anxious about my new behavior, he was reacting to unexpected change the way many of us do—by retrenching and becoming even more set in our ways than we were initially.

If, as recovering parents, we expect our children to jump for joy at our decision not to drink or not to depend on other drugs, if we expect them to congratulate us for our wisdom, to pamper and coddle us through the rough times, to immediately change their behavior and treat us with respect—we set ourselves up for some big disappointments.

Many children will greet our announcement of a decision to begin a chemical-free life with a great deal of joy, but that happiness is often justifiably tinged with a note of caution. Some of us made many such announcements during our drinking days. How can our children know this time we really mean it? They can feel the mixed emotions of gladness that we've finally sobered up, and uncertainty at what the future holds for them as a result of our new direction. Sometimes our kids are very happy about our decision, but they simply don't know how to act when we're sober. They may fall back into old patterns of behaving, and at times it may seem like they are trying to get us to drink again.

If there were a way to work all of A.A.'s Twelve Steps in the time it takes to read them, the inventor of the "speed-sobriety technique" would be extremely wealthy. But no such process has been invented, and unfortunately, as chemically dependent people, patience may come to us only with difficulty. We must work seven whole steps before we begin turning our attention outward and begin making amends to other people. If we jump ahead and skip steps we're more apt to make hollow promises than real amends. We're faced for a time with knowing what we must do, but not yet having the inner strength to carry it out. Our children may be in the same predicament. Our relationship with them doesn't magically change the day we pour the last of the bourbon down the sink or flush those final pills.

We need to *earn* respect and trust from our kids, and rarely do we get those pats on the back when we're lacking in self-respect, self-trust. At the time we make our decision to stop our chemical abuse, we are at a low point in our lives; we've hit bottom. Unless we're superhuman, we don't bounce right back out from one of life's deepest potholes in one graceful leap. It took us years to fall in and dig ourselves deeper. It will take time to climb out again. When we use all our energy jumping up and down, jumping from Step One to Step Eight and falling down, we don't learn self-respect.

The vulnerability most of us feel initially makes it very tempting to want our children to take care of us. Take away our old security blankets and we *do* want to be babied. Wouldn't it be nice if we never had to get out of our rut, if other people would anticipate our needs and meet them? We have a difficult struggle ahead of us and, recognizing that, many of us secretly want to be carried uphill. That way we won't have to face our emotions and learn to express them. We won't have to analyze our needs, try to meet them, and realize that some of them can never be met to our satisfaction. We won't have to practice assertiveness. Unfortunately, we may want to be carried uphill on our children's backs and feel disappointed when they don't take care of us. What's wrong with them? Don't they love us?

The plain truth is that our children can't drive us to drink and neither can they keep us sober. They can't break us and they can't make us. Love has nothing to do with it! When we demand that they make our needs the center of their lives, we aren't making any real gains or changes; we're merely substituting one dependency for another. Our current struggle for a sober life is personal and private. We can and should communicate what's happening inside us to our kids, but we have no right to ask them to make our struggle their responsibility. They have their own burdens to carry. To double their load is to risk bending their backs permanently.

There are several ways we can deal with standing on our own two feet and not becoming overly dependent on our kids and spouses to be our cheering sections during the next days and months. When we feel an attack of the "self-pities" coming on we can run, not walk, to the nearest A.A. meeting to refuel ourselves with the courage to remain sober. We can find and create our own support networks. The structure has already been set up for us in A.A., where we find understanding and fellowship. The whole purpose of having an A.A. sponsor is to provide us with healing help during the rougher moments. We may want to weave a larger net by making new friends, renewing old friendships, or beginning therapy.

We can learn to set up reward systems to reinforce our new sober status, reward systems which aren't hooked to our children or our families. If we buy ourselves a paperback book we've been wanting, set aside half an hour for a calming hot bath, or find other small tokens of affection to give to ourselves, we're less likely to need our family's constant encouragement as we change.

Finally, we can make our goals realistic—one day at a time. There's less chance of discouragement if we deal with our sobriety and our changing family relationships in the here and now rather than the future, which seems to stretch out endlessly ahead of us. Break those goals down into steps, baby steps if necessary, and take them one step at a time.

Trials of transformation

All change is stressful. If it will make you feel any better, even people who receive big job promotions or who win the state lottery feel anxiety. Moving, getting married, and having a baby can all be very positive changes, yet they're stressful as well. When we admit we are chemically dependent and finally do something about it, put the plug in the jug or the top back on the pill bottle, we're making a change for the better. It doesn't always feel that way, though. Along with the determination and the happiness, the optimism and the euphoria, comes fear of the unknown which lies ahead of us, moments of self-doubt and discouragement.

Whenever we turn our faces in a new direction, we turn our backs on the old. When we graduated from high school it was an exciting time in our lives, but most of us felt some sadness. We got a little teary-eyed at the friends and the childhood we were leaving behind. Generally when we say goodbye to something or someone, or even an old habit which has become an established part of our lives, we feel a sense of loss and we grieve. A man may want to marry the woman of his dreams more than he's ever wanted anything, but his bachelor party, a wake for his swinging singlehood, is an important mark of transition. Even though it may not make sense in our rational minds to feel grief at the loss of our old alcohol or other drug habits, those of us who have been addicted sometimes feel as if our best friend moved halfway around the world when we stop drinking or depending on other drugs to get by from day to day.

Our children may feel some grief, too, even though they don't put it into words. Our relationship with them may have been frought with tension and anger, far from pleasant, but that relationship was a known quantity. Even if they couldn't count on us, they could count on *not* counting on us! It may not be easy for them to let go of the past and move into the future at the same pace we do.

They often fear the unknown ahead of them as well, and sometimes they fear it more than we do. When we change, we ask, even if not in so many words, that our family members do the same. In order to remain a family, they'll need to adapt to our changes. One of the laws of change is that it invariably brings on more changes. The change circles are ever-widening, like ripples in a pond. Those ripples can be threatening to kids who've had no say in the transformations going on around them. It's easy for them to feel out of control and uncertain of the future.

When John, a twenty-eight-year-old construction worker, finally put down the bottle, his family saw it as a good thing. They weren't prepared for the fact that he'd be going to nightly A.A. meetings or that he'd be developing a close relationship with his A.A. sponsor, a relationship which even John's spouse couldn't share.

While he'd been drinking, John often ignored the misdeeds of his youngster. His son's grades, which were far below his potential, were just another hassle Dad didn't want to deal with. Often he'd intervene with Kevin's teacher and swear that his son had completed his homework when in fact, John knew no such thing. At some level he was afraid the child's teacher might suspect a drinking problem in the home and he needed to protect his addiction from discovery.

In the past John could escape a confrontation with reality by pouring himself a couple of stiff drinks. Now he stopped doing that. As he began noticing his child's problems, he took steps to help him change.

Kevin dug in his heels. Of course he didn't want to do homework when he'd never had to do it before. Neither did he appreciate John's new reluctance to stand up to the teacher for him and cover his lack of effort. It had been fun to listen to Dad call the teacher a liar. The boy felt protected and loved every time it happened. Now he felt angry and confused and he did everything within his power to get things back to normal.

Obviously, John had to drink if the "good old days" were to return. Kevin began leaving "clues" on the counter: Dad's shot glass and his favorite beer mug. He started calling John names in his presence. "Dirty old alkie" was one of his favorites. The boy tried to engage his dad during the evening before A.A. meetings by picking fights so that John would be tempted to remain at home and finish the argument rather than go to his meetings.

Although most kids don't go to such extremes, more than a few of them unconsciously *do* want their parent and their lives to get back to normal. For an alcoholic or other drug-addicted parent to return to "normalcy" means drinking or using once again. This doesn't mean the kids are evil or disturbed; it does mean they're human like the rest of us. Often, simply being aware of that very human undercurrent of resistance to change is enough to give a recovering parent perspective. Knowing that unconscious sabotage can and does happen in the best of families arms you against being taken by surprise and falling back into old patterns before you know what hit you.

It is important to acknowledge your kids' fears about the future and their anger at the changes they don't like. Encourage them to talk it out rather than act it out. At the same time you'll need to demonstrate your feet are firmly planted on the road to recovery; it might be easier to turn back, but you and they are moving ahead—no pain, no gain! Alcoholics need tough love if they are to recover and so do their children. Share with them your awareness that sober doesn't mean grim and joyless. In time, they will learn to accept the sober you and your new lifestyle won't be so threatening to them; *it* will have become the status quo.

Other kids may express a great deal of initial enthusiasm for a parent who stops drinking or using other drugs, only to grow angry and bitter after a few months. They may have unrealistic expectations about just what will happen once a chemically dependent parent is sober. Like some adults, they expect instant perfection, but a child's expectations can be radically different from those of an adult.

When Nathan stopped drinking, both he and his wife expected their marriage problems would immediately dissolve. His wife would stop hassling him about his supposed lack of ambition and he'd no longer suffer from sporadic and temporary impotence. Nathan's kids had a similar mind-set, but they held different expectations for Dad. Now that he'd stopped drinking, money wouldn't be tight any more and they could have all the toys they wanted. Because Nathan would no longer be preoccupied, he'd spend all his free time with them, taking them to the amusement park and the zoo.

Marian, who had been tranquilized to the point of nearly being comatose for two years, had a similar problem. During the time she'd been drug-dependent, she'd burned dinner nearly every night. Because she was now drug free, both her husband and her son expected gourmet meals. In truth, Marian had never been a good cook. She had no interest in cooking and, no matter how hard she tried, she still occasionally burned dinner. The evening meal became a time for silent recriminations.

Just because you've stopped drinking or taking other drugs doesn't mean you'll become a corporate president, drive a Mercedes, fill the house with video games, or win awards for your cooking. It only means that the substance of your addiction no longer controls your life and that you've taken control. Although you probably will be able to do better at work, and although you may begin to develop previously undeveloped talents and interests, you won't become a completely new person. Simply the fact that you ceased to drink won't bring riches and fame dropping at your feet.

When a recovering parent's kids harbor unrealistic images of a grand and glorious new life, they set themselves up for disappointment. Such fantasies are often impossible in the real world, but when a person believes the fantasy strongly enough, they feel deprived, cheated, and even betrayed when the impossible dream doesn't come true. Most of us become embittered when we see ourselves as cheated or betrayed. Out of bitterness we may react with hostility. Our kids are human and they're no exception.

The best way to handle unrealistic fantasies is to expose kids to reality rather than protecting them against it and let them build recovery castles in the air. Talk about your goals and hopes. Ask your kids their expectations for family life from this point forward. When you keep lines of communication open, you have a chance to correct misconceptions before they harden into rigid expectations. Be open about chemical dependency making sure your kids are aware of just what the problem is and what recovery entails. Sit down with them and help them sort out the possible from the impossible dreams. If they're old enough, you might want to take them to an open A.A. meeting so they can see that other recovering alcoholics come from all strata of society, that recovery isn't necessarily synonymous with riches, fame, beauty, and power.

Testing, 1, 2, 3!

When a parent changes, chances are at least some of the limits will change. When Jerry was drinking, it didn't bother him if his kids slammed the back door and yelled in the evening when he was sufficiently "zonked out" not to hear it or care about it. Loud noises did bother him in the morning, and his kids were required to tiptoe about the house while Jerry gagged down his coffee. Now that he's stopped drinking, his tolerance for noise has changed. The loud evening banging and shrieking bothers him, but he isn't upset by a moderate amount of noise in the morning. When Jerry drank, he swore and couldn't really say anything about his children swearing. Now he's not drinking or swearing and their profanity irritates him.

In the midst of trying to maintain sobriety, Jerry hasn't given much thought to what he wants from his children and how to get their co-operation. He only knows, "they're driving me bananas!" Until he redefines just what constitutes acceptable noise and what constitutes too much noise and sets clear rules for them to follow regarding uproar and cursing, his children must play a guessing game, testing to find out just where Jerry draws the line.

When behavior which a substance-abusing parent might

have tolerated, ignored, or encouraged suddenly becomes taboo, kids can be confused. Children need limits, and they need to know just where those limits are drawn in order to feel secure. Is it okay now to swear when they've hurt themselves? How about when they're simply excited? What about including curse words in normal conversation for shock value? Is it all right to use curse words as a part of their normal vocabulary? Come to think of it, just which words *are* okay to use and which are absolutely taboo? The rules vary from home to home and from parent to parent within a home.

Since most children are more action- than talk-oriented, their first impulse usually isn't to ask you just what your new expectations are for them, now that you've stopped using alcohol or other drugs. The simplest and most effective way for them to discover the new limits you have set for them is to test those limits. What are the rules now? How much have they changed from pre-sobriety days? Do they change from situation to situation? Are they consistent? Does one parent have a higher level of tolerance and a different set of rules than the other? Which rules do they hold in common? What happens when I upset one parent, but the other one thinks what I'm doing is okay?

Kids who aren't aware of their limits often get into trouble with adults. They're frequently punished for breaking a rule they didn't know existed. At the same time, without the comfort of knowing that adults are in control, kids can feel frightened. They aren't always capable of drawing their own lines for their behavior and they may feel as if they are zooming out of control.

The rules of behavior we establish for our children are complex and often change. Take, for example, telling the truth. We instruct our very young children to always tell the truth, but as our kids get older, we tend to modify that rule. It isn't okay to lie, but then it isn't always okay to tell the truth either. Overweight Aunt Martha may look like a beached whale in her new bathing suit, but we either say nothing or we compliment her. In some instances, telling the truth may be labeled as tattling. No wonder limit-testing can be such a full-time job for many children! The changes may come so fast and the rules may be so vague that they have a difficult time keeping on top of new family policy.

Recovering parents who want to minimize limit-testing need to establish new limits and communicate them to their offspring in clear and simple language. It takes a while for kids to unlearn old behaviors which have become habits, so the new rules will need to be restated to them. They may test the limits to see if you really do mean business or if you're just talking out of your hat as adults sometimes are known to do. If you were inconsistent about your expectations and about how you followed up misbehavior while you were chemically dependent, your children will learn that you intend to be consistent only through experience— sometimes oft-repeated experience.

The important thing for a recovering parent is not to take this testing personally. Some children break rules in order to determine whether or not a parent really cares enough about them to notice. Because so many of us were almost completely absorbed in our addictions, we may need to consciously let our kids know that we do notice them, we do care. If a child feels neglected and ignored, punishment becomes validation, a way of saying, "I know you exist."

When this happens, recovering parents need to acknowledge their children's presence in appropriate ways, and to make certain there is plenty of opportunity for positive interactions. It is much more satisfying as a parent to set aside fifteen minutes for a quick game of tag, a shared snack, or a talk than it is to demonstrate caring and concern through a scolding or a spanking.

Sometimes children can feel abandoned and frightened when we go away to A.A. meetings. "I used to wait for you on the porch when you'd go to A.A. meetings and to the counselor," Dylan tells me. "I'd be crying inside and scared that you'd never come home again." If my sobriety was to work, if it was to be long lasting, I needed to meet *my* needs. It was difficult for Dylan to understand I wasn't leaving him for good and I would come back to him. I needed to get away and take care of my personal business in order to really be there for him as a sober parent.

Younger kids may fantasize that a parent is going off to drink instead of seeing a counselor or attending an A.A. meeting. Sometimes, when a parent needs to spend time in detox or an inpatient facility, the children can become extremely frightened about potential abandonment. It is important to be sensitive to a child's fears even though they may not be spoken out loud. Give reassurances even when they aren't asked for. (We adults also often have a rough time asking for comfort when we are afraid someone important to us is leaving!) It may help to leave the child in the care of relatives or friends he or she is familiar with rather than picking a new child care arrangement at this time. Kids may be more comfortable initially if someone watches them in their own home.

"You kept coming back to me, so it wasn't so scary after a while," Dylan explains. And so it is for most children. Some parents will, out of necessity, have to hire a brand new sitter for a child, or leave that child with relatives for an extended period of time in order to achieve strength in sobriety. It can be very painful to leave a child who is frightened, but recovering parents need to weigh a child's temporary anxiety over the long range goal of sobriety. If staying with the child and missing a meeting puts your sobriety in jeopardy, you do your child no favor.

Myths that make our journey perilous

Whenever we plot a new course and cover unfamiliar territory, it isn't hard at all to take a wrong turn and become lost. When we operate under a set of false assumptions, we increase our chances of making time-consuming and energy-depleting detours. Hopefully, after wandering around in circles for a while, we'll end up right where we started and try another route. But by making ourselves aware of some of the common wrong turns other parents have taken on the road to family recovery, we can avoid making the same mistakes.

What are the myths which can imperil our sobriety?

1. "Time alone will set my family right again." Time is an important factor in family recovery and many of the things we've discussed so far do take time. But the passage of time, alone, doesn't guarantee your relationship with your children will improve. Left to chance, relationships can deteriorate over time as well as improve. Time is only one ingredient in the recovery process for parents and children, not the entire recipe.

2. "Stopping drinking will solve all of my family's problems." Stopping drinking or using other drugs is a start, and probably is the most crucial thing you can do. When you are drinking or using it is nearly impossible to solve family problems. Some problems you and your children face today came as a direct result of your addiction, but others were in place before the chemical dependency began. Other problems can come as a direct result of addiction, but in time they seem to take on a life and direction of their own. When you quit drinking you don't instantly solve all of the problems which confront you, but you do make it much easier to work on problem areas and reach solutions.

3. "I can make up to my kids for my past behavior to them." Falling into this trap makes it extremely tempting to buy children out and avoid setting limits. Other parents set limits which are too restrictive in order to make up for an overly permissive history with their children. Going overboard in either direction won't erase what went before

and is a way of still living in the past. You can't take away the past, but starting today, you can begin shaping the future.

4. "If I just try hard enough, I'll be able to solve all of my family's problems very quickly." Expecting too much too soon is setting yourself up for failure. You also make it likely that you'll feel a good deal of anger and resentment toward your children for not following your program and timetable for them. The next thing you know, you'll feel like throwing in the towel. Easy does it! The longest-lasting changes take time.

5. "My spouse is the parenting expert. It's better if I take a back seat." Taking on the responsibility of being an involved parent can be difficult if you weren't that involved during your drinking or drugging days. It may be easier to let your spouse continue to parent alone and to avoid an active role. To convince yourself that avoiding being an involved parent is better for your kids is a rationalization. All parents make mistakes and you will make a few, too. It simply comes with the job. The biggest mistake of all is to give your kids the impression that you don't care, that you can't be bothered to be their parent.

* * *

Philosophers assure us there are several ways of obtaining knowledge. We can be told something. We can experience it. We can intuit it. We can intellectually accept it. We can feel it superficially and then, at long last, we can completely accept something as being true. Our children come to know our sobriety on many levels. We tell them we aren't drinking any longer and over time we show by our actions that we aren't drinking. Each day we progress further in our journey, become stronger in our sobriety, and each day our children know a little more deeply that, yes, we're changing, that sobriety is just as much a fact of their lives as our addiction was.

As human beings, we tend to be creatures of habit.

Recovering parents sometimes fall back into old patterns of thinking, feeling sorry for themselves and toying with the idea that maybe, just maybe, one little, teeny drink wouldn't hurt. Children of recovering parents sometimes fall back into old habits of thinking and relating, as well. Old ways of coping may have become automatic to them, much like pouring yet another drink was a reflex action for us. We can't give up when we catch ourselves going backwards and neither can we give up on our kids when we see them reverting to old behaviors. Learning curves are seldom smooth. Deciding to chuck everything because of one bad day or even a bad week as a parent makes as much sense as giving up on sobriety because we've experienced one slip-up. Each day is a new beginning, a chance to start anew. If we didn't believe that, we'd have no reason to face our addictions and go forward without the pills or the booze.

Even when our road is filled with unforeseen switch-backs and we stumble over a few unexpected rocks and into a few potholes, we and our children are headed in the right general direction and that's what counts.

FIVE

Creating a New Family Environment

Whew! In the beginning there's so much to do that it's difficult to establish priorities and stick to them. Newly recovering parents aren't always accustomed to breaking big goals down into small tasks and deciding which things need to be done first. Our main priority in the past was getting and staying intoxicated. Now we need to come up with a new set of goals and priorities for ourselves and our family so we can create a new family environment which will provide for the needs of our children and our own needs, too.

The complexity of sorting out the tangled threads of our lives and our kids' lives can be overwhelming. If we aren't sure about what we're doing, or if we plunge ahead without studying our problems and noting what needs to be done one step at a time, if we take the steps in reverse order or leave some of them out, we're left with a bigger, more complicated knot than the one we started with.

First things first!

Our primary goal right now and for the days ahead is to become and remain sober. Sobriety and a drug-free lifestyle is the only foundation on which we can build a solid future. Even though researchers Billings and Moos discovered that when parents stopped abusing alcohol their children seemed to bounce quickly back to adjustment, they also found that relapses in parental drinking have very negative effects on the way children see their families.[1] There is conflict between parents in relapsed families, and family members report a breakdown in communications and less emphasis on independence, ethics, intellectual and cultural activities, and recreation. The gains children make during a parent's recovery can be quickly lost during a relapse.

To avoid a relapse, it is essential we learn to take care of ourselves. When we lose sight of this and begin putting the needs and wishes of other people ahead of this, we find ourselves stressed-out, angry, and resentful, and we soon fall back into our old, sick thinking patterns. Nobody cares about me. They just don't understand. I have only one friend in the world—the substance I'm addicted to. We go on a dry drunk and before we know it, we've crossed the line again and the dry drunk has become a wet one. We've forgotten just how critical it is to keep living our lives without being controlled by alcohol or other drugs.

Being concerned about our sobriety isn't the same as being narcissistic or egocentric. Granted, it is something we must do for ourselves and not for other people (attempted sobriety for our spouses' or our kids' sakes, seldom lasts!), but our quest for and commitment to a chemical-free existence does have benefits for those around us, especially our children. Meeting our own basic needs and learning to understand and care about ourselves, being our own best friends, short-circuits this sick thinking. We can no longer say nobody cares about us so what the heck, because *we* care about ourselves and we aren't about to hurt ourselves by drinking or using.

In the beginning, recovering parents need to attend a

[1] Moos, Rudolf H. and Andrew G. Billings, "Children of Alcoholics During the Recovery Process: Alcoholic and Matched Control Families," *Addictive Behaviors,* Vol. 7 (1982) pp. 155–163.

number of A.A. meetings. Sometimes their children won't want them to go. There may be times when it will be impossible to take the kids on an outing to the amusement park or a hockey game where beer is readily available. To put yourself in proximity with alcohol would be tempting fate. Maybe two days or two weeks into sobriety you *can't* show up at Cousin Fred's wedding reception where the liquor will be flowing, even though your spouse and children may be begging you to go and Cousin Fred threatens never to speak to you again if you don't attend.

As recovering parents learn to manage stress, it becomes clear they can't be all things to all people. Some nights after a hard day at work, you don't have the strength to be emotionally on call for the kids. Sometimes you just can't be a homeroom mother or soccer coach. One of the most important skills a recovering parent can learn is to say no and not feel guilty about it.

Occasionally, recovering parents talk themselves into missing an A.A. meeting or getting involved in a situation they know they probably won't be able to handle "for the sake of the kids." They rationalize and use their children as an excuse to put themselves in situations where there will be a big temptation to drink. "I couldn't help it; I *had* to because of my kids," or "I was so worn down by their demands, I couldn't stop myself from drinking," are examples of alcoholic thinking. Recovering parents who put their sobriety in jeopardy for their children's sake and then blame their kids for their slip-ups are still controlled by addiction and denial.

Then too, parents, recovering and otherwise, who have low self-esteem and think they don't deserve to come first once in a while, who believe everybody else should be taken care of before they can take care of themselves, teach their kids a harmful lesson. Children either learn to expect someone will wave a magic wand and meet their every need just like dear old Mom or Dad does, or they may model their behavior after that of their parents and fall into the habit of taking care of others without ever learning to take responsibility for meeting their own needs. Unless we have self-esteem, we can't build our kids' self-esteem.

We *can* take care of ourselves without depriving our children! First we can learn to sort out our needs from our wants. A world cruise isn't crucial to our sobriety no matter how badly we might want to take one right now. Attending A.A. meetings is a need even though we may not want to go. Our basic needs as human beings are the same as our children's, with one thing extra—the need to get and stay sober. Most of the time our needs won't conflict with our children's. When conflict does occur it is frequently temporary.

Our children can gain from knowing we are concerned about their needs, but that we can't always fill them on demand. Part of growing up is learning to delay gratification. If we can't meet our kids' needs now, we can schedule a definite time to deal with those needs later. We can help them learn to solve problems by sitting down and discussing how they might meet their own needs or find other adults who can help them.

Sometimes amazing things begin to happen when parents back off a bit and focus on themselves some of the time instead of making sure the kids are always happy. Four-year-old Barbara may learn to make herself a peanut butter and jelly sandwich on her own if Mom doesn't drop everything and come running at her first sign of hunger. She's learning to take care of herself and take pride in her new responsibility. If Dad doesn't run to school and cuss out the principal over thirteen-year-old Billy's lunchtime fistfight with another student, Billy will learn how to deal with adult authority figures on his own.

It isn't easy to let go, to find the proper distance from our children's lives. Occasionally we may have to remind ourselves that our kids have a need for independence, too, although they may want us to carry them. It is hard to recognize our own needs as valid if we feel we have to make up for our less-than-adequate parenting in the past.

Putting our needs ahead of our children's means that sometimes they'll have to wait. It isn't neglect, cruelty, or abuse to tell a child, "I can't talk with you right this instant because I need to call my A.A. sponsor, but I'll be glad to talk with you later this evening or tomorrow." We *are* being neglectful if we ignore our children's needs completely or invalidate their feelings and desires. It is possible for us to be assertive and let them know we care at the same time. "I know your friends are important to you, but I've had a terrible day and I need some peace and quiet right now. Let's find a time when you can have them over. Tonight isn't it."

SAYING "NO" RESPONSIBLY

1. Acknowledge the child's request.
2. Acknowledge the child's *feelings* about the request.
3. Clearly state your feelings. Don't plead, overexplain, or try to reason.
4. Say no.
5. If the request is negotiable, set a time for more discussion or set a time when you'll grant the request.

When necessary, we'll explain to our kids why *our sobriety* must come first for us. We can do this in a way which doesn't shift the responsibility for our sobriety to their shoulders. Many children of chemically dependent people, although they may not express the anxiety in words, believe they are the ones who caused their parent's addiction. Telling a child, "If you don't stop bugging me right now, I'm going to get drunk," is damaging. A child can cave in under the blame heaped upon self-blame which is already burdensome, or that child may decide, "What the heck. I'll keep right on bugging you so you'll go ahead and get drunk and be out of my hair!" or, "Well, you're going to get drunk anyway, so does it matter what I do?" Such power is a double-edged sword and one which children shouldn't be given.

It is crucial for recovering parents to own the responsibility for their own sobriety and to tell offspring what is needed from them without blaming or accusing. "I'm feeling a little uptight right now and I need you to give me half an hour alone," serves the purpose well. Another way of putting it might be, "When you keep interrupting me and insist I pay attention to you right now, I get upset and nervous. Please find something to do on your own for half an hour and then we'll get together and talk." Avoid "you make me" statements at all costs. Your children don't "make" you do anything. You choose how you'll react emotionally and respond to their demands.

There are other ways we can take care of ourselves besides learning to say no. We can:

1. Take time to attend A.A. meetings, alcohol education seminars, and counseling sessions. Understanding and support outside the immediate family are essential to solid sobriety. Your children don't force you to stay home. (There have been no recorded instances of kids tying a parent to the bedpost to prevent that parent from attending an A.A. meeting!)

They may try to make you feel guilty and manipulate you out of going. "If you loved me, you'd stay home tonight." You may feel like making your children feel guilty or manipulating them into giving you permission to go. "I'm doing this for you and you don't really appreciate it." Instead of fighting dirty or using the kids as an excuse to remain home when you really didn't want to go out anyway, it's much simpler to regard your attendance at A.A. meetings or counseling sessions as a given. Make child care arrangements. Tell them when you're going and when you'll be home—then go! Your sobriety depends upon it.

2. Develop hobbies and interests to fill the time previously spent drinking or using. Because you may feel at a

96

loss initially as to how to spend all that time on your hands, it may become tempting to make your kids an all-consuming passion in your life, to become so involved that they're in danger of smothering from all your concern and attention. When parenting becomes an obsession or an attempt to undo a past which can't be undone, you need to step back and take a long, hard look at what you're doing.

Your kids are individuals and separate from yourself. Although you can guide them and help them grow to be the kind of people you'd like them to be, you don't have total control over how they will turn out. Even when things are going well, they will still disagree with you at times and they'll still disobey you. They'll want friends and interests of their own. Remember, independence is one of their needs! If you measure your own self-worth solely in terms of what your children do or don't do, you can end up feeling angry, alone, and betrayed.

Find things you can take pleasure in doing alone, with your spouse, or with friends. Your children should be a big part of your life, but not all of your life. As you begin exploring new facets of yourself and rediscovering old interests which your addiction shoved aside, you'll find your confidence and sense of self-worth growing. That can't help but improve your parenting. Becoming a vital and interesting person also helps you put your role of parent in perspective.

3. Learn to monitor your feelings. When we were under the influence, many of us didn't pay much attention to our feelings, except the sensation of craving another drink or needing to be sedated. Some of us grew uncomfortable at the first twinge of feeling and we tried to cure our anger, fear, sadness, or jealousy by blotting it out with drink or other drugs. But drinking and using other drugs don't cure negative feelings and they don't make fear disappear. Instead, chemical substances serve as a Band-Aid. When we're covered with Band-Aids, we don't necessarily know that

beneath them, our hurts have been festering. Once we stop drinking or using drugs and peel off the bandages, we may be shocked at what we see, what we finally feel.

We can learn to pay attention to the hurts and do something about them while they're still twinges, rather than leaving them alone and letting them grow and spread unchecked. Some of us, however, still choose to ignore our feelings. We deny their existence, only to have them emerge after they've grown to monstrous size.

Our self-pity blossoms and soon we're surrounded by a jungle full of anger and resentment. Our road to recovery is so overgrown we can't even tell whether or not we're on it or off. We're lost. That isn't the way to maintain sobriety or to stay on top of the job of parenting!

If your children are doing things that upset you, tell them now rather than waiting until you can no longer contain the explosion building inside you. Monitoring your feelings and dealing with them as they arise, rather than resorting to overkill or drinking when you can't take it any more is a matter of sobriety survival.

United we stand

Although some recovering parents are raising their kids alone in single parent homes, others have a spouse in the house and need to learn once more how to parent as part of a team. Often alcoholism or other drug addiction weakened bonds of affection and trust between ourselves and our spouses. Before we can expect a secure home life, we need to reestablish our relationships with our marriage partners.

When alcohol or other drugs assume enough importance to become a family member, everyone is affected, and that includes the people who are married to the chemically dependent person. Sometimes husbands and wives become hooked into a denial pattern, blaming everything but the addiction of a spouse for family problems, covering up and protecting, justifying the abuse. Spouses frequently use the same adaptation tactics as children of alcoholics do. Some withdraw, others become super-competent and take over the addicted spouse's functions and tasks in the household. Spouses can act out and rebell by having affairs, getting drunk, or threatening suicide or divorce. Studies show that established patterns of dealing with life and with other family members can become extremely rigid in chemically dependent households. Change, learning to work as a team, may come slowly for both the recovering parent and the spouse.

Maura felt compelled to make up for lost time when she stopped drinking. She felt bad about how she'd pulled away from her husband and her children during the last months of her drinking. As soon as she was released from the inpatient facility where she dried out and received counseling for two weeks, she plunged back into her role as mother. Immediately she tried to "reform" her kids with the energy of a zealot. No, they couldn't eat cereal for dinner anymore; she would cook well-balanced meals. No, George couldn't sign up for baseball because his grades had dropped and he needed to study. No, Susan couldn't spend all of her allowance on make-up.

Maura's husband, who'd seen to family details during his wife's heavy drinking, had other ideas. It was fine with him if the children fixed cereal for dinner sometimes. George really should be on the baseball team and how Susan spent her allowance was her business. Before long Maura and her husband were engaged in an all-out struggle for control. George and Susan, in the meantime, soon realized they could take advantage of this parental warfare by playing Mom and Dad against each other. Tension escalated and before long Maura began sneaking drinks in order to escape a family where everyone seemed against her.

Power struggles between parents often develop out of misunderstandings. Lines of communication need to be reopened between recovering parents and their spouses *before* new expectations are expressed to children in the home. Part of the job of parenting is to provide family leadership. If parents are at loggerheads over how the children should be raised, an atmosphere of confusion, tension, and insecurity is created.

The task at hand, consciously setting family goals and priorities you and your spouse feel good about, isn't a simple one. It does offer you, your spouse, and eventually your children an opportunity for growth most families never have. Generally two people get married, they have a child and maybe another and another. Family rules and roles just seem to grow like Topsy until it seems as if "we've always done things this way and we can't change." A chemically dependent family must change if it is to recover. Parents are given an extra push to see whether or not children's needs are being met, to reflect on their values and how they plan to transmit those values to their children. Rather than being locked into rigid patterns of doing things, parents can look at their options and make choices.

Undoubtedly you and your spouse will have some differences of opinion. You need privacy in which to work through those differences and come to a compromise each of you can feel comfortable with. When your children are in the room or even in the next room with little ears glued to the crack in the door, there's a big chance for misunderstanding, anxiety, and manipulation. The adults are in charge here (or they will be shortly) and they need to get their act together *alone.*

Recovering parents need to set aside time with their spouses to talk through parenting issues and make plans for problem solving before problems arise. Pick a time when both of you are relatively relaxed and when you're not busy. It is critical that you take this time without the children, even if that means running away from home with your spouse to a coffee shop or the park or shipping the offspring to Grandma's for the day.

Conflict is a healthy part of dynamic relationships be-tween vital individuals. If you and your spouse agreed on everything, there wouldn't be much point in talking—you could read each other's minds. Come to think of it, there wouldn't be much point being together. The boredom would be unbearable. We all have different tolerance levels when it comes to what we're willing to put up with in our kids. We have different notions of how our kids should be raised based on the way our own parents raised us. To ignore conflict doesn't make it disappear. The object of our summit meeting with our spouse is to air those differences of opin-ion and discover the common ground we share.

Both you and your spouse might want to begin by taking a few minutes alone to make a list of the things your kids do which bother you. Because you and your spouse aren't clones, the lists will be different. Start by making a column headed "It Bothers Me When My Children:" and freely write down everything which comes into your mind, the major hassles and the nit-picky irritants. Do strive to be concrete as you make your list and focus on behaviors (things they actually do) rather than attitudes.

Single parents will find they can clarify their own expec-tations for their children's behavior by making a list, too. If you are a single parent, you won't need to negotiate with another adult, but you will find it helps to grab some quiet time away from the kids to work through the process of formulating family rules.

If you need some inspiration, perhaps a look at the sam-ple list will provide some for you. Now you're ready for column two: "I Wish They Would Do This Instead." Care-fully note a positive behavior you wish your children would substitute for each negative one you've noted.

Congratulations! You and your spouse have just com-piled a first draft of the new family rules. But you're not finished yet. There's more to do before you rush to nail both lists to the front door. First you need to show your lists of grievances to each other. If you find items you've

IT BOTHERS ME WHEN MY CHILDREN:	I WISH THEY WOULD DO THIS INSTEAD:
1. Don't clean the tub after bathing.	Clean the tub right after they've taken their baths.
2. Slam the door so hard pictures fall off the walls.	Close doors quietly.
3. Borrow my clothes without asking and return them soiled or not at all.	Ask permission before borrowing my clothes and return them promptly in the conditon they were in when borrowed.
4. Whine!!!!	Ask for things in their regular voices.
5. Watch T.V. 6 hours a night.	Watch T.V. 1 or 2 hours a night.

both listed, place a star next to them. Now discuss each of the other items on both lists point by point. Does a particular item seem important to both of you? If it's a thorn in the side of only one parent, just how important is it to that parent?

Part of this exercise is to get parental gripes out on the table as a way of opening up communication and allowing yourself a catharsis of sorts. Now we've got to get down to the job of editing. (Like it or not, first drafts invariably need editing!) Expecting our kids to obey 679 new rules isn't realistic. In the first place, the front door isn't big enough to serve as a bulletin board for all those sheets of paper. In the second place, even if our kids are geniuses, they can't possibly break a huge number of bad habits all at once.

Do save your first drafts so that you can come back to them in a month or so and see if the house rules may not need another revision. Sometimes the items we thought were critical aren't that important in retrospect. At other times the trivial becomes critical with the passage of time. And as our kids master one set of behaviors we can *slowly* help them master others.

Now together with your spouse, combine the items on

each list and number them according to just how important they are to you. Again, you may not agree with your husband or wife. That's okay. Aim to create a top ten list of pet peeves. (If your children are very young, you may need to trim the list even further.) Some items, the starred ones, will be easy ones to include. The remaining items will need to be negotiated. "Cleaning someone else's bathtub ring really disgusts me. If you'll let me have that one, I'll concede to your gripe about the top being left off the peanut butter jar which really doesn't bother me much at all."

I keep a quote from John Wayne taped to my kitchen cupboard to remind me that the best rules or reprimands are short, sweet, and to the point: "Talk low, talk slow, and don't say too much." As you combine your lists, weed out the extraneous and make a final copy, using simple language and short, easily understood sentences. Working to clarify and simplify now means you won't be caught up in shrill, nagging tirades and explanations later.

No parent likes to nag. As a matter of fact, no child really enjoys being nagged either. (Dylan tells me nagging is just a mother's way of whining!) Somehow, in the process of family limit-setting, nagging, pleading, cajoling, begging—even whining—seems to creep in and set a negative tone. That's why it's a good idea to make a "public" copy of the family rules, the copy for your children's eyes. You and your spouse have dealt with both the negative behavior and the positive alternatives to it in your lists. The new family rules will accentuate the positive:

FAMILY RULES
1. Clean bathtub right after you finish using it.
2. Close doors quietly.
3. Ask permission before borrowing another person's belongings. Return them promptly and in the condition you found them.
4. When you want something, ask for it in your regular voice. No whines please!

5. You can watch two hours of T.V. a night *after* you've done your homework and chores.
6. Put jar lids back on tightly after you use the peanut butter.

Why family rules? Children often become legitimately upset and even belligerent when they see themselves as victims of a bunch of "bossy" adults. Family rules are a way to set limits so family members can live together peacefully. They don't single out one person. This kind of limit-setting establishes rules for children *and* adults. It isn't fair to expect our kids to clean the tub after us when we forget to do it ourselves. Family rules help establish an attitude of cooperation rather than conflict.

There's another good reason for establishing family rules. When we can agree with our spouses on discipline, we stop our children from playing one parent against the other before it starts. These aren't Mom's regulations or Dad's demands; they are a joint statement.

Certainly, they won't cover every single contingency. Because of differences in our children's ages and capabilities we need to be somewhat flexible and able to deal with and discipline each child spontaneously, too. Just because we've established family policy doesn't mean our kids will confine themselves to the misdemeanors on our lists. When five-year-old Ralphie finds a book of matches on the sidewalk and brings them home to test the flammability of the curtains, he needs to be disciplined even if you didn't see into the future and include a ban on arson in the family rules. Even so, family rules can be a good way to handle both your teenager's blasting stereo and your toddler's pot and pan banging in a nonthreatening, nonblaming manner.

Next it's time to agree with our spouses on specific consequences for the kids when they violate the rules we've just established. Logical consequences which flow from a child's behavior show our kids that they have control over what befalls them, by closely linking our reaction to their action—they made a choice to break a rule. Fair and logical consequences are aimed at having a child take responsibility for the rulebreaking and they mirror the reality of life.

When a child whines we don't feel like listening and we don't want to do things for or with that child for a while. (We'd feel the same if it were an adult whining, interrupting us, or butting a head into our stomachs!) A logical consequence for whining might be a 15 minute "timeout" for the child in his or her room. Logical consequences teach. A "timeout" for irritating or petty antisocial behavior teaches children that people don't want to be around them when they act this way.

A child who borrows our things and then forgets to return them or returns them in bad condition, can face a ban on borrowing for a week or even a month. Chances are, during that time there will be some things the child wants, be they the scissors or that new perfume you just bought. By standing firm, we teach our children that when they don't act responsibly toward other people's possessions, people don't lend them things anymore. At the end of the borrowing ban, the child has another chance to show that he or she can now handle taking care of other peoples' belongings.

When children refuse to pick up after themselves, parents have a couple of logical alternatives. The first is to interrupt whatever the child is doing and direct the child to pick up immediately. The second might be to do the job yourself, but to keep the toys or whatever you've picked up for a set period of time.

Chores fall into two catagories. First there are those which only affect the child. Then there are those which affect other family members. Family responsibilities need to be listed right along with the rules, so children know exactly what is expected of them. Younger children in a family won't have many chores, but the youngest child can do something, even if it is only dusting and picking up his or her toys. As children become more able they can take responsibility for cleaning their rooms, taking care of family pets, doing dishes, doing some cooking, and other more complicated tasks. Even though kids may never admit they like to do chores, participating in the family work does give them a sense of belonging. Learning to take responsibility for themselves helps them gain independence and build self-esteem.

It is not fair to be vague when you tell kids you expect them to pull their own weight around the house. Be clear about exactly what tasks you expect them to perform and let them know the job specifications ahead of time. The first time you have a child do a new task, do it together so you can show the child your expectations. What does doing the dishes entail? For some families, it may mean cleaning the counter, the sink, and the stove, as well as clearing the table and putting the food away. In other families doing the dishes, means just that: doing the dishes. For the young, novice dishwasher it can easily be interpreted as using cold water and bubblebath. Unless you clearly define the job to kids, they don't have much of a chance of doing it well.

Recovering parents may find it difficult to be tough on chores. Typically we feel a good deal of guilt, and there's a temptation to let our kids slide because we've given them such a hard life in the past. After a while we feel anger at being taken advantage of. Resentment builds and we're back into alcoholic ways of thinking. It isn't our kids' doing if we feel guilty. We need to deal with that feeling and take responsibility for it.

Dylan finds it very difficult to put his sweat socks in the dirty clothes. At least every three months he tells me we need to buy new socks because he doesn't have any. After nagging, finding the socks myself, and becoming more and more resentful, I simply put the responsibility for his socks on his shoulders where it belongs. If he doesn't put his dirty socks in the laundry basket, they won't be washed. Perhaps they'll be lost in his room. He'll either have to wear dirty socks to school or no socks at all.

Having been a drinking mom, I shudder internally at the thought of Dylan having to take his shoes off at school and revealing socks so ripe they would be condemned by the health department. What will his teacher think? (Unfit mother, that's what she'll think.) But because I've stood my ground and struggled to work through my insecurities rather than laying them on him, it's never happened—not once! It seems that he, too, cares what his teacher and class-mates might think, and dirty socks can be downright un-comfortable. They make your feet itch! So when he's run out of clean socks, he finds the dirty ones, and if it isn't a regular wash day, he throws them in the washing machine and does them himself.

Some chores affect the whole family. When it's a child's turn to do the dishes and they aren't done, usually there's a fight or somebody else does them. The same holds true for taking out the trash and that all-time least favorite job—cleaning out the cat box. Some parents may feel comfortable using the no-work-no-play tactic. "You can't watch T.V. until you do the dishes." Other parents choose to pay kids for family chores and "dock their wages" when the work isn't performed. Another alternative is to explain to the child ahead of time that in order to participate in family fun, that child must perform family chores. If the cat box hasn't been cleaned and the dishes done a reasonable time after they've been dirtied, the child will be excluded from the next family outing.

No matter what consequences parents devise for break-ing family rules and for shirking family work, they must be fair and based on the degree of acting out, on the child's age and capabilities. Remember, too, that the consequences must somehow be tied to the rule the child has broken so that the child can easily make the connection between the "crime" and the punishment. Smashing a teenager's rock albums because he made long distance calls you didn't approve, or banning dessert for a week when a younger child stops doing chores doesn't teach anything except life is illogical and unpredictable. Good consequences for family rules teach control and they make it easier for our children to develop self control. Both are issues which are very important in recovering chemically dependent families.

Good consequences take some thinking. When a child makes long distance calls, should you have him pay for them out of his allowance or should you buy a phone lock and deny him use of the telephone for a time? That will depend on your family. Consequences vary from family to family just as workable family rules do.

One good way of approaching consequences is to imagine what would happen if your children broke a particular rule in the world outside your family and to adapt that consequence to your family. Household chores are a child's equivalent of an adult's job. What happens at work when you don't show up, fail to carry out assigned tasks, or do them, but don't do them well? Do your superiors excuse your poor performance, do they cover for you, do they nag and end up doing your job themselves? Sometimes recovering parents find themselves secretly performing their kids' chores and covering up to the other parent. They fall into the trap of enabling their children to avoid responsibility just as their bosses, co-workers, and spouses enabled for them during their drinking days.

Many family rules are aimed at helping members of your family live more easily together. These rules teach courtesy and control in social situations. What happens when adults borrow things from the neighbors and never return them? What happens when adults hit others who don't agree with their political opinions? If an adult goes out for a stated period of time and comes home many hours later, then complains about eating a burned dinner, how do others react? What consequences come from those reactions?

Protecting children from the consequences of their actions deprives them of responsibility for their behavior. There are too many adults who don't understand why people don't want to be around them and who have a terrible time changing their behavior because they never learned as children that impoliteness and thoughtlessness aren't okay in the real world. When kids don't do chores, you can't fire them. When they aren't pleasant company, you can't divorce them, nor would you want to. You can set appropriate consequences which will help them change their behavior so that when they grow up, they'll find employment and form relationships, and so they'll be good parents to their children.

Another factor you'll need to take into consideration is what to do about first offenses, and fifth and sixth offenses. Old habits aren't always easy to break. You may want to establish a warning for the first time a rule is broken and a very mild consequence the second time, say a five minute time-out for the child. The third time a rule is broken, a fifteen minute time-out might be appropriate. It's a good idea to start fresh, especially with young kids, every day. Some children have a need to test, and if parents keep escalating consequences with no new beginnings, those children risk being sentenced to their rooms for life. A standoff is established and, in order to save face, parents and kids are locked into a rigid cold war. Finally the consequences have escalated so far it's impossible to enforce them.

Once you and your spouse (or you alone, if you're a single parent) have agreed on consequences for your family rules, write them down. It can be difficult to remember them in the heat of battle. It is also easy to forget, two days or two weeks from now, just what consequences you agreed to. "I thought we were going to send them to their rooms." "Well, I remember we were going to take away the T.V.!" Often, when you get caught up in conflict with a spouse about what you agreed to do, the argument over who is right and who is wrong escalates and disciplining the kids is forgotten.

Make a pact with your spouse or with yourself, if you're a single parent, to consistently enforce the rules with the consequences you've set out. In two-parent households, and in stepfamilies especially, it is critical for both adults to agree not to undermine the other parent in front of the children. There will be times when you think your spouse is acting like Atilla the Hun and your urge is to "save" your kids from the consequences, especially if the other parent has been the family disciplinarian in the past. On the other hand, your marriage partner may resent your new input and might unconsciously try to minimize your impact by undermining your efforts to discipline.

Agree to back the other parent up and get an agreement from your spouse to back you up unless the situation borders on physical violence. As soon after the incident as possible, make time together (away from the kids!) to talk it over in private and come to an agreement. Occasionally you or your spouse will treat your children unfairly. You'll discipline them for things they didn't do or, in the midst of anger, yell and enforce consequences which are too harsh, given the circumstances. You're human. Your spouse is human. Neither of you can make correct judgment calls all the time. You can present a unified parental front to your kids and minimize the chances of too much unfairness by keeping communication open with your spouse.

Laying Down the Law

Now it's time to set forth the new rules to your kids. One of the best ways to do this is to hold a family meeting. You might want to begin by saying, "We've talked over some things we think will make our household run more smoothly and we came up with some family rules."

110

Share the job of going over the family rules point by point with your spouse. Remember, these aren't Mom's rules or Dad's rules; they are *family rules*. Although you may want to explain your reasons for some of the rules, avoid blaming. "If you kids weren't such creeps, we wouldn't have had to make these rules," isn't going to gain their cooperation. At the same time, be aware that the rules, your expectations for their behavior, can become buried in lengthy explanations.

Be sure to use clear and precise language. The whole purpose of explaining the rules is to be understood. As parents, we sometimes expect our children to read our minds. One night Dylan, his stepdad, and I were watching T.V. During the love scenes he insisted on making loud kissing noises. "Behave!" I snapped at him. He gave me an angry and bewildered look. The minute the next mushy part appeared on the screen he was making the noises again. This time I defined the behavior I wanted him to stop. "Quit making those kissing sounds," I told him. He stopped. Frequently we use verbal shorthand and our children aren't certain what they're doing wrong. We owe it to them and to ourselves to communicate clearly.

Expecting our children to agree to the family limits we've set defeats the purpose of limit setting. Let your kids know that the rules are a given, a fact of life, but that you are open to questions about the interpretation of the house policy and about the consequences. By discussing the "what-ifs" now, you can avoid the "I-didn't-knows" later. If your kids begin asking questions like, "When you say washing clothes, do you mean shoes and belts, too?" resist the urge to be judgmental and respond with something like, "Boy, that's a stupid question!" Instead, firmly steer the conversation back on track. When kids are uncomfortable, they tend to get silly and stop communication. If you become judgmental, you give them a perfect excuse for clamming up.

Once you're fairly certain everyone understands both the new family rules and the consequences for breaking them, it is helpful to post a copy in a highly visible place. (We use the refrigerator door in our house.) With family rules in black and white and handy for future reference, it is easier for kids to stick to those limits and for parents to enforce them.

Children may insist that the family should be democratic and they may ask for more input than you're willing to give. Complete democracy rarely works in families because all family members aren't equal in maturity. Input *is* a good idea, but it can be difficult to handle in the beginning. For most recovering parents and their children, creating a cooperative rather than a conflict-oriented family environment is a big change. Unless someone exercises leadership in times of transition, the family can founder. At this point putting that leadership on your children's shoulders, even when they ask for it, is forcing them to play the role of parent.

Family members need to gradually learn how to cooperate, how to solve family problems. Even though it may be tempting to try and solve everything at the beginning through discussion (it sounds so good!), the give-and-take will take time. Sometimes children have a hard time communicating. When the issues are emotionally charged there's a big chance for conflicts to erupt which can't always be resolved. Anger and resentment have a way of blocking problem solving.

If parents tell their children everyone in the family has an equal say in how it will be run and then go back on their word, kids may feel lied to and betrayed. Setting up a situation where the kids decide how you'll spend your family vacation is an example of misguided family democracy. Suppose they vote to go to Disneyland and you don't want to go there. You're stuck paying for a vacation you don't want and feeling resentful, or you're put in the position of negating their decision. "We aren't going there under any circumstances!" It is better to come up with one or two acceptable choices when it's appropriate and then let your kids choose between two or three things you can live with. Sometimes having kids make choices won't be appropriate.

The very fact that you're holding a family meeting rather than a lecture can give children a sense of "we're all in this together." Another good way to help them feel included is to give them input about family chores. Together, as a family, you can list the jobs which need to be done around the house and how often they need to be done. Then make a chart of who is responsible for what jobs. Family members can learn to communicate and accomplish something together. It can be fun to use different colored marking pens and symbols. When the chart is finished, you'll have visible proof that you can do problem solving together as a family.

After you've established the ground rules and both you and your children have lived with them for a time, you might want to ask for feedback at future family meetings. Kids may have their own ideas about rules which could make the family work better. Often parents may wonder why they didn't think of those things themselves. Allowing this sort of input helps them in the transition from external controls to self-control. Older children can be very good at brainstorming consequences, as well. Parents can formulate acceptable choices so kids have some say in how the family is run. To give children complete control in family matters leaves their needs for guidance, external control, and security unmet.

By starting small and setting realistic goals for family meetings, you insure some success. Too many failures at the beginning and before long everyone is ready to quit and go back to the old ways of doing things. The rules didn't work because there were too many of them and some of them conflicted. The kids voted on the consequences and because they outnumbered you, they vetoed consequences and instated rewards for rulebreaking. Rather than discussing, your family ended up blaming and insulting each other and even the family dog had to leave the room.

One step at a time may seem slower, but at least you know where you're going and you stand a good chance of getting there in one piece.

SIX

Dealing With Feelings

When we drank or took other drugs we buried our feelings beneath chemicals. Deep inside us, these feelings simmered and bubbled. When our emotions did burst out we had little or no control over how they were expressed. Some of us lashed out and became verbally abusive over the hurts we thought others had given us. Others of us became depressed. We cried and talked of taking our lives. When we were sober we acted like normal people, but when we were drinking or drugging we acted out our negative feelings in primitive ways.

For others it was difficult to express love and caring when we weren't under the influence because we felt too vulnerable sober. We protected ourselves from being used or hurt by acting like Oscar the Grouch sober and Ms. or Mr. Congeniality when we were in our cups. Wearing the armor of a mood-altering substance, we allowed ourselves to be playful and affectionate. We laughed and hugged and made friends easily with other drinking or other drug-using buddies.

As our drinking progressed the mood swings became more frequent and more out of our control. We might get drunk in order to get something off our chest and end up frightening and alienating people or even having ourselves arrested for being drunk and disorderly. Perhaps our affectionate and playful moods turned into bed-hopping or playing the fool people laughed at rather than with.

From watching us, our kids learned that feelings were larger than life, uncontrollable and frightening things. While our own alcoholic resentment and anger at the world and ourselves was growing, our children felt some highly uncomfortable emotions, too. Some of them were terrified for their safety or frightened of being abandoned by us through being rejected or even death. Others predominately felt anger. How could we be doing this to them? Deep sadness is another emotion which is common in alcoholic homes.

There were times when they felt affection, but it was difficult for them to express it to us, because there was no telling how we'd react. Our reactions depended almost entirely on how much we'd had to drink or how many other drugs we'd taken. Sometimes even seemingly inconsequential events, words, or gestures would trigger a storm of rage from us. Or we might overreact in the other direction and become maudlin or embarrassingly affectionate. So our kids learned by experience as well as example that it was better to stuff feelings inside or even to deny having them than risk the consequences of emotional openness.

Our addiction controlled not only our lives, but the lives of our family members. Hopes became dashed after we'd broken promise after promise. Our spouses began feeling cheated, angry, sad, and betrayed. They, too, often kept feelings inside. Because we had so much invested in denying our addiction, it became very dangerous for our families to express what they felt. To examine a feeling, to express it, or even to have it, meant possibly having to face up to the disease of alcoholism or other drug addiction. If they haven't obtained outside support from counseling or Al-Anon groups, families tend to be hooked into denial right along with the chemically dependent family member. It isn't enough to deny the disease, they soon deny their feelings, too.

116

For me, drinking and feeling was like attempting to drive on a mountain road knowing I didn't have any brakes. I had control during the first part of the trip, the uphill journey before I'd managed to get drunk, but once I'd reached the crest and started zooming on the hairpin twists and turns of the downslope, I went totally out of control. With each passing second my speed increased and my ability to steer lessened. The scenery started going by so fast my vision blurred. If something got in my way I crashed right through it as if it weren't there. The guardrail meant nothing. It took large objects and painful impacts to stop me.

During my sober moments, I shuddered at the things I'd said and done. "You just can't trust your feelings," I'd tell myself, mistakenly believing it was the emotions and not the drinking that was my problem. That made about as much sense as deciding to outlaw all automobiles because some don't have brakes rather than passing a law to insure that all cars on the road have working brakes. I convinced myself that I was emotionally ill, a certifiable crazy, and that I should be locked up. Many alcoholics have similar experiences. When you are trapped in the middle of denial it's easier to label yourself insane than to even consider life without liquor.

After a time of driving without brakes, chemically dependent people and their families learn to be very careful and try to seek out level, straight, emotionless roads at all costs. To do otherwise would seem foolhardy. Now that you and your family are on the road to recovery, it may be difficult to remember that the brakes work again, that if you're gathering speed, you can slow down by using another method besides smashing into something. The emotional hills, curves, and bumps in the roadway may make your journey a bit rough at times, but because you are in control they won't send you crashing off the road.

It takes time to get over the fear of having an emotional accident because you were out of control in the past. For a while you and your children and spouse may feel as if you're walking on eggs around each other. Not all family members will be comfortable either with facing their feelings or with sharing them at the same time. Prying, pushing, and prodding by the recovering alcoholic can drive family members even further into their protective silences.

It is very difficult for people to be open about their feelings unless they trust the person they are sharing them with. As we've said before, trust is earned slowly; it can't come instantly. Often children's trust level for their chemically dependent parents eroded a good deal during the course of the disease. Expecting family members to instantly be experts at openly sharing their feelings, or even wanting to share their feelings, as soon as the drinking or drug using stops is unrealistic.

Two months into sobriety, Maxine felt frustrated and stymied by her family's inability to communicate. She'd been learning to be open and honest at A.A. meetings and she longed to have the same type of emotional give and take in her home. She called her husband and her three children together for a family meeting.

"I know you all feel angry at me for my drinking behavior," she began. "I want you to tell me about it today."

No one replied.

"Bobby." Maxine focused her gaze on her eldest son who was staring at the floor and shifting uncomfortably in his chair. "You can't help but feel a lot of resentment toward me and I want you to tell me about it."

He shrugged his shoulders. "I dunno."

In turn, Maxine grilled each of her family members about the anger she assumed they felt and received equally noncommital answers. Finally, after a frustrating hour of getting nowhere, she gave up and her husband and children left the room as quickly as prisoners being released from jail.

At first she felt sorry for herself. Because they wouldn't

tell her how they felt, she was certain that they must hate her even more than she'd originally guessed. The self-pity quickly turned into anger and resentment. If they cared at all about her sobriety, they'd open up, damn it. If they didn't care, neither did she. She'd given them their chance and they'd blown it. She wasn't about to put herself in that position again. If they didn't feel like talking, they could just keep their feelings to themselves.

Unfortunately, Maxine in her eagerness to rush communication, skipped several steps and her family feelings meeting was doomed to fail before it began. She hadn't recognized that it had taken *her* many A.A. meetings before she was comfortable discussing how she felt with other people. She had forgotten that in the beginning her feelings had been so threatening, she'd denied having them. In her rush to get everyone in the family talking, she'd put them on the hot seat and told them how they felt. No wonder they reacted with guarded wariness.

Getting to Know You

A good part of the trust-building process entails getting to know the person you're supposed to trust. Often, chemically dependent parents withdraw from their children and when they do engage them, they are unpredictable and moody. A recovering parent may be a virtual stranger to his or her children even if that parent has spent a great amount of time in the physical presence of those kids. In addition, sobriety is a new twist, something children may not be accustomed to at all.

Just as children of recovering parents may feel they don't really know their parents and can't guess how they will react, recovering parents often don't know their children. Because so much time and energy was taken up by alcohol or other drugs, there was little left over for relationships— including those with the kids. It isn't unusual for recovering parents to feel that their children are strangers to them. If the kids have withdrawn or spent most of their time outside the home and avoided the chemically dependent parent, this feeling of alienation can be even more intense.

The first step in opening up communication and in dealing with feelings is to get reacquainted with our children. Comfortable relationships aren't established overnight. Getting to know them again, and allowing them time to get to know us, works best if we start by sharing nonthreatening feelings and activities. We need to make time to reestablish our relationships with our kids on an individual basis. Family togetherness is fine, but children need contact with us on a one-to-one basis, too.

We can work to build comfortable, trusting relationships with our kids by:

1. *Doing things together with them both individually and collectively.* For most children, heavy heart-to-heart talks are difficult to handle initially. Task-oriented situations give both parents and kids something to do when the silences become awkward and tense. When a parent and child run out of small talk, there isn't pressure to perform because you can turn your attention to the task at hand, whether it be looking at the animals in the zoo or washing and waxing the car. Talking about what you're doing at the moment may not be the deep, revealing sort of conversation you crave, but it is a good start at communicating.

Outings with individual children can be a lot of fun and they show that child that he or she is special and deserves attention. But, as visiting divorced fathers will attest to, outings can become artificial and stilted after a while; there's very little relating at a movie. As you look for activities to do with your kids, seek out more everyday ones as well as the entertaining ones. One idea might be to plan dinner, shop for the ingredients, and cook together. (Even very young children like to make pizza!) Yard work, painting, and other household projects offer opportunity for both problem solving and conversation. Reading out loud, fixing a bike, or playing catch are good possibilities, too.

2. *Showing an interest in our children's opinions.* Kids need to be shown that it's okay to have opinions and to express them, even if those opinions don't match yours. When talking about feelings is too threatening, opt for easier topics of conversation. "What do you think about the new T.V. series we watched last night?" "Which do you like best, baseball or football? Why?" "Blue's my favorite color. What's yours?" If children are reluctant to engage in conversation with us, we can ask them open-ended questions, those which require more than a yes or no for an answer. When we seek out our children's opinions we demonstrate that what they think, who they are as individuals, is important to us.

3. *Listening and responding to our children in a nonjudgmental way.* It does little good to ask a child to share an opinion with us if we don't listen to the reply, or if we discount it with a judgmental comment. Few things turn off communication faster than, "Boy, that's a dumb idea!" or "You don't know what you're talking about!" When we were drinking we were often inattentive and too wrapped up with ourselves to listen. Two good ways to let kids know we're listening to them is to maintain eye contact with them and to rephrase what they've said and respond with that after they've finished. "So you like blue best of all?"

4. *Sharing our thoughts and feelings with our children.* Opening ourselves to our kids is another way of showing them it's perfectly okay to have opinions and thoughts and to express them. By starting with topics of conversation which aren't emotionally loaded, we can model ways of having differences of opinion, of disagreeing, without hurting other people, or invalidating what's going on inside them. "Well, I have to say that pink is my favorite color, but blue's nice, too."

Sometimes it takes many such tentative conversational forays before children will be ready to tackle deeper emotional issues. They may need to be reassured over and over again that speaking out won't earn them punishment. Many

121

recovering parents need to take the opportunity to get to know their kids, to learn to spark conversation and listen, to keep the conversational flow going by giving encouragement, and being nonjudgmental in their responses. Communicating with children is a skill and it takes practice, but it can be learned. That learning process can be fun in and of itself. The more you practice with your kids, the sooner good two-way communication will become second nature to both you and the children, the sooner you'll be able to feel fairly comfortable talking about emotions.

Once More With Feeling!

Now that you and your children have been able to make communication headway, it's time to begin learning how to honestly express emotions, and teaching our kids how to do the same. Sometimes getting children of chemically dependent parents to open up is a slow process. By now your kids should be aware that it's okay to communicate nonthreatening issues, but they still may fear landmines in the road which might be set off by feelings.

As Maxine quickly found, putting children on the hotseat, telling them what they feel, or playing interrogator more often than not has the opposite effect from the one you intended. It is better for both recovering parents and their children to start talking about feelings on a one-to-one basis. Parents can slowly introduce some "feeling talk" into their conversations with kids.

It is important to remember you aren't a family therapist and even when you, your spouse, and the children are able to handle emotional family meetings, you aren't running an encounter group or a therapy session. You are trying to share how you feel and to help your children do the same. You're working at dissolving the old denial system, giving everyone in the family a chance to know where the others are coming from, and eliminating guessing games.

Young children, or children from families where chemical dependency has been a family member for an extended period of time, may not even have an emotional vocabulary. How can you talk about feelings when you don't have any words to express them? Psychologists Melvin L. Silberman and Susan A. Wheelan in their book, *How To Discipline Without Feeling Guilty,* suggest working on a joint language with children. They explain, "The more certain words and expressions are shared, the more clear communication tends to become." Some words we might want to teach our kids as we start communicating emotional states are: resent, tense, left out, put down, confident, control, responsibility, trust, threatening, and defensive. As you think about communicating with your own children, perhaps you can come up with others.

Even the simple words like anger and love can be confusing. My "anger" might be irritation because I erased a disc on my word processor by mistake and had to retype thirty pages. Yours could be a boiling, furious rage because I said something which hurt you deeply. Yet we use the word "anger" to describe both levels of feeling. Love, too, has many meanings. I love my child. I love my husband. I love eating popcorn at the movies. In each case, love means something different.

One way a recovering parent can help keep feeling communication lines clear of misunderstanding is to help children become aware that the same "feeling words" can mean a number of things. You can make a game out of seeing just how many shades of meaning you can come up with for words like happy, sad, angry, love, jealous, and nervous. When you are talking about feelings with your children, it's a good idea to ask, "I'm not quite sure what you mean by depressed. Could you explain it to me a little more?" even when you think you know what's being said. Teach your children, too, to ask for clarification.

We communicate feelings, not only through words, but through facial expression, voice tone, and body language.

We need to make ourselves and our children aware that the content and the feeling of communication can be miles apart. Comedian Steve Martin is far from repentant or polite when he says, "Well, excuuuuuuuse me!" A good way to become more aware is to play an acting game with your kids. Write down a few simple sentences on slips of paper. (I'm so happy, I could dance for joy. Please pass the salt. What time did you get home last night? All of the sides and angles in an equilateral triangle are the same.) Now pass the hat and have each child draw a slip. As family members call out emotional states like sadness, nervousness, rage, sarcasm, or joy to the "actor," have that child say the statement with feeling!

Focusing on feelings can be fun when it's done with a light touch in the beginning. Nonthreatening games are a good way to reassure our children that everyone has emotions and that it's fine to express those emotions; we aren't going to hit the roof. Through play, both children and recovering parents can start to become aware of more ways of talking about feelings and ways of nonverbally expressing them. Such games also help children loosen up and feel comfortable with their own emotions. Expressing themselves in front of other people won't be quite as frightening as it was before.

As recovering families, we're getting used to having brakes again, learning that we are in the driver's seat and can control how we feel. Our emotions aren't going to run away with us. Because we're in control, we need to learn to take responsibility for our feelings, to own them.

When Dylan comes home from school, throws his jacket and backpack in the middle of the floor, and bellows, "What's to eat?" while I'm right in the middle of an important article, I feel angry. I don't like it when he is demanding and uses an impolite tone of voice. I become irritated when he tosses his belongings on the floor for others to trip over them. The irritation bubbling inside of me is *my* feeling.

He has not *made* me feel anger. His actions may have triggered a process inside of me which causes anger, but there are other ways I could feel. Anger is *my* response to his actions.

As chemically dependent people we often blamed others for our disease and our feelings. We wouldn't drink if the kids didn't make us so damned upset. We wouldn't have to take tranquilizers if the boss didn't make us grovel to him for a raise. Blaming is one of the major steps in denial. Chances are our spouses and our kids began to blame *us* for their problems and negative feelings. We learned to preface our complaints and feeling statements with blame. "You make me so mad I could scream." "If you didn't drink, I wouldn't feel so miserable."

Blame and damning accusations are very potent. One of their side effects is selective deafness in the hearer. The blame comes through loud and clear, but that's where the communication screeches to a halt. When someone accuses us of something, especially something we didn't do, we get our hackles up and become defensive. Right away we've got to come up with a good defense. We're so busy trying to defend ourselves from the attack, we never listen to how the other person is feeling. That part falls on deaf ears. Blaming nearly guarantees we won't be given a fair hearing. It's self defeating.

As part of our own recovery we need to own up to our emotions, to take responsibility for our feelings. That's what making an inventory is about. We made a list of *our* defects, not our family's defects, or our employer's defects, or even the defects of the economic system and the government. In the Sixth Step we were ready to have God remove these defects, not the defects of our spouses, our children, or the man down the street who insists on cranking up the power mower at six in the morning on Sunday.

Emotions are not defects, but blaming our feelings on those around us is defective thinking. When we use it, we become victims. Since we certainly aren't about to look inside ourselves and admit we have responsibility for our emotions, we must rely on other people to change for us. We give them the blame, but we give them all the power over how we feel, as well, and we lose in the bargain.

When we take responsibility for our feelings we can communicate them responsibly. We'll say, "I feel angry," rather than "You make me angry." We help our children learn to own their feelings and communicate them appropriately by cleaning up our own act first. Instead of holding in our feelings, we'll communicate them without blame to those around us. When our kids see how we handle feelings, they will be able to follow our lead. We can show and we can tell, too, taking the time to explain to them the importance of using "I statements."

Parents whose kids are accustomed to talking about their feelings can't always wait passively until the offspring initiate a discussion. Children find some issues very difficult to talk about. Even when they understand that a parent isn't going to laugh at them or react with anger, fear of embarrassment can bottle emotions. When our parental antennae tell us something is wrong because there's a sudden change in our children's attitude and behavior, we owe it to them and ourselves to check out the underlying feelings which go with the change. Kids who can't or don't talk it out often act it out instead!

Often we can get our kids to open up to us if we arrange a quiet time alone with the child and say something like, "I've noticed that you've been quiet lately and keeping to yourself and I'm concerned that something's wrong." While our children may need some urging to talk about how they feel, including reassurances, encouragements, and open-ended questions, it's important to respect their privacy and not to pry or intrude where parents don't belong.

Another way to help children start to talk about what's bothering them is to notice reactions they may have during a family conversation, or even while they're watching a T.V. show, and use their comments as an opening. Five-year-old Ned became upset while watching an episode of a T.V. sitcom which dealt with drinking problems. He jumped up and began running around the room, punching sofa cushions, and talking in a loud voice as if to drown out the program.

"I see watching this show upsets you," his mother began.

"It's a dumb show; a stupid show," he countered loudly.

"Lots of children feel bad when they remember how it was when their parent drank. Maybe you feel bad when you think about when I was drinking."

Hugging him, she drew him into her lap and, with a little more encouragement, Ned began letting out some of the pain he'd been storing inside.

When children feel embarrassed about their feelings, they may need permission to have them. Ned's mom's statement about lots of children helped Ned to know that he wasn't bad or strange. Other children shared his feelings; he wasn't alone. Sometimes, when communications begin to falter, a parent can help things along by making a statement about other boys and girls or many teenagers. When children are old enough to attend, Alateen or Alatot meetings can also show them that other children have shared the experience of living with a chemically dependent parent, and that other children have also experienced some of the negative feelings they have.

When kids clam up, or when they seem to take forever to say what they're trying to say, we parents are often tempted to put words in their mouths and interpret their feelings for them. "You hate me because I was a drunk." "You're just jealous of your sister because she gets A's and you don't." There's a world of difference between "I think this may be what you're feeling. Am I right?" and "You're feeling mad at the world." The former is a question, a way to get information from the child. The latter is telling the child what to feel. Unless parents possess rare psychic abilities, they can never be certain of what emotions their children are experiencing until the children tell them.

When we guess at our kid's emotions and toss our guesses back at them as if they were statements of fact, we're frequently off base. Maybe Jeff doesn't hate you at all because you drank; he is mad because you ordered him to eat all his broccoli last night. It could be that Susie isn't jealous of her sister; she had an argument with her boyfriend and she's upset about that. Sometimes we look back on our own childhoods and confuse what our children are feeling now with what we felt then. When we mislabel our children's feelings, we run the risk of having our children accept our diagnosis either to please us or because it's easier to comply with our interpretation of their emotions.

We need to encourage rather than discourage our children when they talk with us. We encourage them to open up by giving them lots of eye contact, and by nodding, smiling, and giving them verbal cues to keep talking like "uh huh," "yes," "then what happened?," or "how did you feel about that?" We can restate what they've said, so they know we're listening and we can try to bring out their feelings by commenting on voice tone and gestures. "You sound as if you were really frightened." "You're bouncing up and down so much right now, it seems to me as if you're nervous."

Parents discourage communication by lecturing, minimizing, or discounting their children's feelings and by labeling. Communication is a two way street. When we do all the talking and our kids can't get a word in edgewise, they quickly tune out what we're saying and we never learn what they're feeling.

Often parents minimize their children's emotions with remarks like, "I don't see why you should be upset about *that*" or, "Wait until you grow up, then you'll see how silly you're being." Even though from our perspective as adults the cause of a child's pain may seem trivial, the child doesn't feel pain any less acutely than we do. Just because I'm not concerned about someone stealing my comic books, that doesn't mean my child isn't. His comic books are as important to him as my T.V. set is to me!

Labeling instantly cuts off communication as if you'd flipped off the switch. Words like "dumb," "stupid," "silly," and "crazy" have no place in conversations with children about their feelings. When we use them, we give our children a double message: I want you to tell me how you feel/I don't want to hear it! Even when we feel anger at what we hear from our kids, we can find better ways to deal with that anger than to put our kids down for their emotions.

Occasionally, we may find that no matter what we do, our children simply refuse to talk with us. Dana Cogan, a Denver psychiatrist who has worked with adolescents for ten years suggests, "Then talk with your children about why it's so hard to talk about feelings. You may even have to talk with them about how hard it is to talk about how hard it is to talk about feelings, but eventually you will reach a place where they'll be able to open up."

Sometimes we *will* feel angry at our children. There are times when family meetings can erupt with emotional conflicts. How we handle our disagreements with our kids sets the climate of our relationship with them. Can we agree to disagree and learn to fight fair or will we engage in battles so bitter we'll lose sight of what started the argument?

Rules for Fighting Fair

When we handle them well, arguments can pull family members together and actually strengthen relationships. Unless family members are able to express their anger, they either hold it in and nurse grudges or act it out in inappropriate ways. Without conflict and dissatisfaction there is no change. Families become stuck in a rut and don't grow. Arguments can be constructive or destructive—it all depends on how we conduct them.

1. *Keep in mind that the purpose of a healthy argument is to solve the problem which started it in the first place.* In the heat of battle it is easy to lose sight of that ultimate goal and to pull out all the stops in order to win. When families look at arguments as ways to resolve conflict there aren't any losers.

2. *Stick to the issue at hand.* When family members are bent on winning, it's tempting to switch subjects and read off a whole list of mental grievances. Even though it may be possible to silence the other person by attacking from several directions at once, when you do it, you make problem solving nearly impossible. Nothing throws reason out the window quite so quickly as character assassination. The purpose of a constructive argument isn't to list every single thing wrong with the other person or to prove that they're insensitive, an idiot, or worse.

3. *Keep it in the present.* Most of us have lived with our families for a long time. Chances are, during that time every family member has occasionally goofed up. Arguing about what went on back then, be it two months or two years ago, isn't speaking to what's happening now. The discussion quickly is diverted to past events, events you can't change or make go away. Feelings are hurt and tempers flare, but nothing is accomplished.

4. *Own your feelings.* Use "I statements" as you express your feelings and avoid blaming, namecalling, and labeling. "I'm really angry because I've done the dishes every night this week and we agreed to divide the work. What are we going to do about it?"

5. *Listen.* Planning what you're going to say while the other person is still talking is cheating! You can maximize communication and understanding while diffusing anger if you use some of the same techniques you do when you

want to encourage your kids to talk about feelings: eye contact, restating what they've said, noticing and commenting on feeling content. Try not to interrupt. If you feel you aren't being given equal time, you might want to use an egg timer or appoint a family time keeper so that everyone has a say in the matter.

6. *When you feel an argument is going out of control, you can put on the brakes by finding something, anything, in what the other person has said to agree with.* You don't need to concede a major point or tell a lie. You can say something like, "I can see how you would feel angry at doing the dishes every night." By showing that you are hearing what they say and that you are making an effort to understand, you can help break down the barriers to problem solving which uncontrolled anger creates. You shift the argument from the level of attack/counterattack to one of cooperative conflict.

7. *Avoid absolutes.* (Absolutely!) In the heat of anger, it may sound good to say "You never," or "You always," but such exaggerated statements are rarely true. When you use one, you escalate the argument, and push it further from the realm of problem solving.

8. *If you feel your rage building to the point where you are afraid you can't control it, or if you find yourself feeling frightened of the other person, agree to take a timeout.* It is important to come to agreement on this rather than dramatically storm out of the room. Set a limit for the "break." Five or ten minutes usually works well. Take a walk and cool off while other family members do the same. It's important to try and calm yourself during the timeout, rather than brooding and letting your anger build. Now come back to the family bargaining table and try it once more.

9. *Be willing to compromise.* Look for creative solutions to family conflicts. Rarely will a solution please every family member, but in all probability you can reach some type of a resolution which all family members can live with. Finding solutions to family conflicts is important because

when there's no agreed-upon solution, families tend to have the same argument over and over again. Tension builds, feelings are hurt, and it becomes more difficult to talk and listen rationally.

Reaching Out for Help

Sometimes recovering parents find it difficult to build appropriate and safe outlets for talking honestly about family feelings. Maybe we just don't feel competent, we've driven so long without brakes or turn signals or even windshield wipers so we could see where we were going that we need driving lessons. Perhaps our children or marriage partners just won't cooperate with us in creating a new, emotionally honest, and open family environment. Sometimes A.A. simply isn't enough.

One of the major keys to recovery in the A.A. program is to reach out. Before we can live productive chemical-free lives, we must reach out to a Higher Power for help. Recognizing that we can't do it on our own is critical. Finding we're unable to walk the road to family recovery on our own is nothing to be ashamed about. There must be plenty of others like us, families who need a bit of assistance in getting back on the right track. Otherwise there wouldn't be so many social workers, psychologists, psychiatrists, and chemical dependency counselors listed in the Yellow Pages!

We aren't thinking too clearly if, once we realize we're lost, we refuse to ask directions from people who know the terrain. Because recovering families are unique in some of the problems they share, it is important for us to seek out expert help from professionals who have training and experience in both chemical abuse and family therapy. Divorce and stepfamily counseling are also new specializations in the helping professions and single parents and stepfamilies may want to explore these options.

Asking directions from the wrong people can lead a recovering parent and his or her children even further off the recovery path. Family therapists who have no education about chemical dependency can ignore critical issues completely and be blind to the dynamics which operate in many chemically dependent households. By the same token, there are chemical dependency counselors who aren't schooled in family therapy. They feel competent with the recovering parent, but they don't know how to handle the kids or the marriage partner. Anyone living in a stepfamily will tell you there is a whole other set of dynamics operating there, too, and a therapist who tries to make a stepfamily over into something it is not and never can be does more harm than good.

Family therapy is just as important as a car or a house or even a refrigerator. It makes sense to shop for help and to shop wisely. Recovering parents and their families can find counseling referrals from:

———Friends in A.A.

———The local chapter of the National Council on Alcoholism

———The state psychological association

———Nearby medical schools

———In- and outpatient treatment centers at local hospitals

When you call to set up an appointment, it is perfectly acceptable to ask the therapist his or her credentials for dealing with recovering nuclear families or stepfamilies. Find out how much the therapist will charge. If you think you've found help, then go ahead and make an appointment. The first session is usually devoted to intake. Some family therapists prefer to work with the recovering parent alone at first. Others start with couples counseling and still others like to see the entire family from the beginning. Be sure you understand who is to come to this first appointment.

During the session you and the professional have a chance to size each other up. By the end of the hour, you should have some idea of the techniques this particular therapist will use and whether or not you and your family can work with that person effectively. Therapeutic relationships depend in good part on trust. If you feel put off, doubtful, or have any questions, the time to resolve them is now. If you're satisfied you and your family will find the kind of help you need, you're all set.

If not, call the next helping professional on your list. Keep trying until you find help in finding your way as a family again. Already you've passed a number of milestones on the road and with some assistance you can keep right on gaining ground. There's no reason to stumble blindly in circles when you can choose to get help and get on the right track again!

SEVEN

Talking With Our Children About Alcohol and Other Drugs

Many recovering parents find discussing alcohol and other drugs with their kids just as embarrassing as talking with them about sex. Alcoholism and other drug addiction are emotionally charged topics for us. Sometimes we mistakenly convince ourselves that because our children have seen us grapple with addiction and win, we can skip the heavy discussions. After all, haven't they seen enough of the ravages of chemical dependency firsthand to know better than to take chances with alcohol and other drugs?

Not necessarily! No one knows exactly why, but children of alcoholics and other drug abusers may run a higher risk of developing the problem themselves as they reach maturity than do kids who don't have a chemically dependent parent or parents. Chemical dependency runs in families. An estimated fifty percent of alcoholics have an alcoholic mother or father, and according to Dr. David L. Ohlms, a research associate at Washington University's Social Science Institute, when one counts uncles, aunts, brothers, and grandparents, the figure rises to a dramatic ninety-five percent. A child's risk of crossing the line between social drinking and alcoholism increases with the number of blood relatives who are alcoholic and the severity of their disease.

Studies conducted on children who were separated from their alcoholic parent(s) at birth and raised by non-alcoholics, have shown that kids with a biological parent who is an alcoholic have a four to five times greater chance of becoming alcoholic than do control children.

Research at the University of Washington in Seattle indicates that children of alcoholics and siblings of alcoholics react more acutely to alcohol than do other people.

A study conducted on adoptees in Sweden isolated two types of parent-to-child alcoholism transmittal. The first, called male-limited, was highly hereditary, passed from severely alcoholic fathers to sons, and environment had little impact on that transmission. The other form of inherited alcoholism, milieu-limited, is passed from parents with relatively mild problems to daughters and sons, and is considered to be a predisposition which can be triggered by the environment. The link between mother-daughter alcohol problems is especially strong in this type.

One of the causes for inherited alcoholism or an inherited predisposition to alcoholism currently being studied is liver enzymes which cause alcoholics to metabolize alcohol differently than nonalcoholics. Researchers have also isolated brain chemicals which determine a person's preference for alcohol. While medical and psychological researchers still have far to go, it is critical to realize that there is probably more to alcoholism than meets the eye.

That doesn't mean all your kids are destined to become alcoholic no matter what you do. Environment does play some role in the development of the disease for some alcoholics. Children model their behavior after the behavior of adults. Kids also formulate values, including those about alcohol and other drugs, based on how they've been raised. When our children have learned to cope with stress by withdrawing or rebelling, they may turn to alcohol or other drugs as escape or provocation. Some children from alcoholic homes grow up to marry alcoholics simply because, to them, alcoholics are 'normal' people. As recovering parents we have already become nondrinking role models. We can help our kids develop sound values, help them find new ways of coping, and teach them healthy ways of relating to others.

What the new research means is that we have a pressing need to tell our kids the facts about alcohol and alcoholism: that it is a disease, that it does have a hereditary factor, and that alcoholics can recover.

Why can't we let the schools do it? Unfortunately, some schools don't have good alcohol and other drug education programs. Even in those states where such educational units are mandated, they're often treated in a cursory fashion, or taught incompetently. Some teachers can't be bothered to put much energy or effort into yet another requirement from higher up. Others feel less comfortable talking about alcoholism than do recovering alcoholics.

We can be our children's best chemical dependency teachers because we have a unique relationship with them. Once we've worked to establish trust, in all probability our kids will find it easier to open up with us and ask questions than they will in a classroom full of peers who aren't aware of the impact alcohol has had on our kids' lives.

We have more opportunity to discuss alcohol and other drug issues with our children than teachers or school counselors do. We can be there to seize opportunities for conversation. More than likely, the opportunities will come to us in the form of a small child checking out our soda with a discreet sip, or a teenager weaving home with strawberry wine on her breath. As we consciously educate our children about chemical dependency we aren't limited to a week-long unit or a one day seminar; chemical dependency awareness in our homes is an ongoing process, just like recovery is.

Finally, we're experts of a sort. We've been there. Although we'll tell our kids the facts and the theories, we've had the experience to know what we're talking about and our children are aware of that. Our personal experience can be their best teacher if we openly discuss it to help our children become more aware of the issues. Passively sitting back and allowing our drinking days to speak for themselves is the same as letting our kids watch hours of T.V. violence without a comment on our part, and expecting them to sort out a system of values regarding violence on their own. We have a duty to help our kids interpret the past rather than leaving it to chance.

While we have a responsibility to help our kids develop solid alcohol and other drug values, we also have a right to anonymity if we choose that. For some of us anonymity is a moot point. Our neighbors, our children's friends, and their teachers are well aware we had a chemical dependency problem. We can tell our children that many people don't understand alcoholism as well as they or we do. To announce to the world, "My parent is an alcoholic," may invite teasing, scorn, and other reactions neither you nor your children are prepared to handle. Some issues are private and personal. You respect your child's right to privacy by not sharing your child's confidences with other people and you expect and deserve the same respect.

It is important, if you decide to keep complete anonymity, not to use it to prevent your children from seeking help outside the family when they need it. Ordering them never to breathe a word about coming from an alcoholic home can stop them from sharing their feelings with professionals and from coming to terms with alcoholism, accepting it as a disease rather than a moral weakness or a curse. If handled improperly, anonymity can turn into denial. Be careful not to institute a blanket gag rule.

We can make alcohol and other drug education a part of our everyday lives by:

1. *Educating ourselves to alcohol and other drug facts.* We can learn more about alcoholism and other drug addiction by reading, attending A.A. meetings, and talking to chemical dependency counselors. Some sources for information are

—Hazelden Educational Materials, Box 176 Pleasant Valley Rd., Center City MN 55012.

—The National Clearinghouse for Alcohol Information, Box 2345, Rockville, MD 20852.

—The National Institute on Alcohol Abuse and Alcoholism, 5600 Fishers Lane, Parklawn Building, Rockville, MD 20852.

2. *Presenting the facts to our kids in a simple and straightforward manner.* Lecturing, threatening, cajoling, and exaggerating distort the facts rather than communicate them. We want to demystify the disease of chemical dependency for our children, to strip it of guilt, blame, and moral judgment. As new converts to a sober lifestyle, we may be more than a bit tempted to play the zealot. When we succumb we run the risk of turning our kids off and losing credibility with them.

Younger kids need to know that alcoholism is a disease and that alcoholics can and do recover. Older children are ready to learn about the progress of the disease, the notion that predisposition is hereditary, and the biological effects of alcohol or other drugs on the human body. Teenagers can be made aware of the warning signs of chemical dependency and are better able to comprehend the dynamics of the disease and the denial syndrome.

We also need to make a distinction between chemical dependency and irresponsible drinking or other drug use, and to talk to our children about the latter as well as the former. Otherwise they can get the impression anything goes as long as it isn't alcoholic drinking or other drug addiction.

3. *Helping our children come to terms with mixed messages they receive about alcohol and other drugs.* Any child who watches T.V. knows that alcohol is the beverage of choice. Even on the sitcoms aimed at kids, characters routinely drink their way through their allotted half hour. Rarely do these shows deal with the consequences of drinking. Watch T.V. with the children and together tally the number of drinks

per show. Talk about why these characters drink, and drink without getting drunk. Discuss T.V. show stereotypes of alcoholics and drunks. Are alcoholics really harmless buffoons?

Look at liquor ads with your children and analyze them. What are the advertisers trying to say? If I drink this brand of beer, I'll be macho. If I buy this kind of bourbon, I'll have men chasing me. Ask them what they think really happens if they buy the brand of beer they can drink all night without getting tired of the taste. What happens if they drink it all night?

4. *Suggesting our children might want to attend an open A.A. meeting with us to see exactly what goes on there.* We can also let them know about Alateen and Alatot meetings and offer to take them.

5. *Finding out about alcohol and other drug education materials and making them available to our children.* Books range from the funny picture book, *The Cat Who Drank Too Much,* [1] by LeClair Bissell, M.D. and Richard Watherwax, and the workbook, *My Dad Loves Me, My Dad Has a Disease* [1] by Claudia Black for younger children, to *The Secret Everyone Knows* [1] for teens by Cathleen Brooks, and *What, When, & How to Talk to Children About Alcohol & Other Drugs,* by Gail Gleason Milgram. [1] You can obtain catalogs which include materials for children by writing

Al-Anon Headquarters. P.O. Box 182, Madison Square Station, New York, NY 10010.

Alcoholics Anonymous, P.O. Box, 459, Grand Central Station, New York, NY 10017.

Hazelden Educational Materials, Box 176, Center City, MN 55012.

National Council on Alcoholism, Suite 1405, 733 Third Avenue, New York, NY 10017.

---

[1] Available through Hazelden Educational Materials, Box 176 Pleasant Valley Road, Center City, MN 55012.

In addition, you can check out the young adult section at your local bookstore. There have been a number of novels written for teens recently dealing with family alcoholism.

6. *Being alert for T.V. specials and episodes of regular shows which deal with alcoholism and other drug dependency in constructive and informative ways.* Recently a number of rock stars have admitted to alcoholism and other drug addiction and have publicly spoken about their disease and recovery. A number of good starting points for discussions with kids abounds if you keep your eyes and ears open.

* * *

Even though our kids may vow they'll never drink, to believe them is to hide our heads in the sand. As many as seventy percent of all teenagers have had a drink. Usually they have their first drink by age thirteen. Twenty-three percent of high school students drive after drinking. And one in three high schoolers rides in a car with a heavily drinking driver at least once a month. Death rates in the teen years are rising dramatically while they decrease for all other age groups. Actuarians attribute this to alcohol and other drug misuse and abuse.

When we think of kids who drink, we tend to imagine teenagers. They are the ones who receive most of the publicity. Yet at many A.A. meetings you'll find a number of people who will tell you they began drinking addictively at about age eight or nine. Some alcoholics began even younger, by sneaking drinks from the family liquor cabinet or finishing half-empty drinks at parents' parties. More than a few of our children may be facing a good deal of peer pressure in elementary school to drink or take other drugs. Others, out of necessity, are latch-key kids and have easy access to alcohol or other drugs at home. Prevention, if it's going to work, must begin early.

It is important for us to let our kids know where we stand on alcohol and other drug use and to avoid giving them double messages. A month after Sam was released from an alcohol treatment center, his teenage children wanted to throw a party. Even though they were underage, they asked their dad to buy beer for them. Sam complied. After all, it was better for them to drink at home where they could learn to handle it rather than drinking somewhere else and driving home. So Sam bought six cases of beer for twelve teenagers and watched them drink it all while he struggled with the impulse to have a brew or two himself. While on the surface it seemed as if Sam was being masochistic, in truth he was getting something from the party—he was getting vicariously drunk through his sons and his friends.

All the wisdom in the talks Sam had given his boys vanished that night as Sam contributed to their abusive drinking by providing the beer. Recovering parents who allow and even encourage their underage kids to drink at home are giving their children a double message. It's bad to drink and at your age drinking is against the law, but it's perfectly fine to drink and I'll even help you.

Parents need to make their teenagers aware of the perils of drinking and driving and to be available to provide transportation for a child in an emergency situation, when getting home would mean either driving drunk or riding with a drunken driver. If the parental taxi service becomes a habit and begins to serve as an enabler, it's time to check out what's going on and to set some limits or get some outside help.

We need to be aware of the factors which may influence whether or not our children will drink abusively. Our *attitudes and actions* toward alcohol are important. When we recover, we become a positive rather than a negative influence. *Peer pressure* has a big impact. If our kids hang out with friends who drink heavily, they will probably conform to group expectations by drinking themselves. *Doing well in school and church attendance* and involvement seem to correlate negatively with heavy drinking among teenagers. New York researchers have found that *parents who are warm, affectionate, and who communicate with their adolescents* have fewer drug using kids than those who are cold and uncommunicative. A father's relationship to his children is especially important.

Some **warning signs** that a child may have a predisposition to alcoholism are: *daydreaming, feeling left out, impulsiveness, being easily frustrated, overactivity, inability to accept correction, and a short attention span,* according to Dr. Herbert Barry of the University of Pittsburgh. Family problems such as separation, divorce, and chemical dependency are often reported by adolescents hospitalized for alcohol abuse. Legal crises, school problems, suicide attempts, and running away from home also frequently precede chemical dependency treatment for teens.

One of the most important things we can teach our children as they move out into the world is the ability to make informed decisions. They need assurance from us that they do not *have* to drink. They can decide to say no. As parents, we can help them gain that ability by roleplaying with them until they feel comfortable with assertiveness. They need to be aware that drinking doesn't make them sexier or more sociable. And they need to know that the consequences of irresponsible drinking can be death through alcohol poisoning or automobile accidents.

Because in the past denial was second nature to us, we may selectively ignore the signs that our kids are in trouble with alcohol or other drugs. We don't do them any favor when we cover up or make excuses for them. We may make it easier on ourselves and on them in the short run, but in the end both we and our kids lose.

Some of the indicators that our children's alcohol or other drug use may be getting out of hand are an overemphasis on parties and a disinterest in schoolwork, hobbies, and activities which used to be important to the child. Mood swings, friends your child refuses to let you meet, argumentativeness, evasiveness, and denial are other red flags.

Not all teenage and pre-teen drinking, even when it's

very irresponsible, is alcoholic drinking. Some kids simply want to belong and go along with the crowd. Others use drinking to rebel, and still others are simply experimenting. But because many of our children do have a predisposition to alcoholism, we have a special responsibility to watch carefully for signs of alcohol abuse in our kids and to take action if we see them.

Taking action doesn't mean calling the child an alkie and staging a screaming confrontation. Neither does it mean playing counselor. Because we've been through this once, we may feel the urge to handle it by ourselves. Suddenly we may find ourselves drawn into all the old tactics our spouses used with us, the blaming, the threats, pouring liquor down the sink. We all know how well those worked!

When recovering parents suspect their child or children are involved with alcohol or other drugs, it's time to get tough and get help. Confrontation doesn't have to be hysterical. "I've been noticing some changes in you and I'm really concerned," is effective. Give the child an opportunity to talk. If you believe the alcohol or other drug use is abusive, make an appointment for the child with a chemical dependency counselor and make certain the child gets there. With professional help you may be able to plan a family intervention. Resources for your alcohol- or other drug-abusing child are available, as well, in the form of teenage A.A. groups and adolescent inpatient and outpatient treatment facilities.

In extreme cases the most loving response we can give a child is a tough one. It may require admitting the child to a detox facility or treatment program involuntarily. That choice is a difficult one for a parent to make, yet the Twelfth Step requires us to carry the message to alcoholics, and to practice A.A. principles in all our affairs. Our kids aren't excluded. Knowing what we know about alcoholism and other drug addiction, having been through it ourselves, to turn our backs on our children and either ignore their alcohol and other drug problems or enable them is negligence of the worst kind.

* * *

As a recovering parent, you've come a long way; your children have gained ground, too. Even though there are many miles to go ahead of you, now you have a better fix on just where it is you want to be and the best route for you to take. Even though some days and weeks or even months may be uphill struggles, you'll find the road smoother and the scenery getting better and better as you go along. Stop to smell the flowers and look around. Getting there can be more than half the fun! Whether the trip is an arduous trek or a challenging and exciting expedition all depends on how you look at it.

We've experienced the misfortune of being chemically dependent. Melville said misfortunes are "something which can serve us or cut us as we grasp them by the blade or handle." When we get a handle on our addictions, our unfortunate pasts can serve us and our children well. We can turn the pain into gain.

Because you've had the courage to stop drinking and travel the road to recovery, you've given your children an important gift: the knowledge that we learn from our errors rather than being crushed by them. That lesson won't erase the past, but it can transform the past and recycle it into something positive—a new beginning.